THE
HBCU
EXPERIENCE

THE HBCU Band Alumni Edition

Visionary Author Dr. Ashley Little
Lead Author Dr. Christy A. Walker
Foreword Author Ashley Maclin

Published By: The HBCU Experience Movement, LLC

The HBCU Experience Movement, LLC

thehbcuexperiencemovement@gmail.com

Ordering Information:
Quantity Sales: Special discounts are available on quantity purchases by corporations, associations, and nonprofits. For details, contact the publisher at the address above.

ISBN: 978-1-7349311-6-7

A Message from the Founder

Dr. Ashley Little

Historically Black Colleges & Universities (HBCUs) were established to serve the educational needs of black Americans. During the time of their establishment, and many years afterward, blacks were generally denied admission to traditionally white institutions. Prior to The Civil War, there was no structured higher education system for black students. Public policy, and certain statutory provisions, prohibited the education of blacks in various parts of the nation. Today, HBCUs represent a vital component of American higher education.

The HBCU Experience Movement, LLC is a collection of stories from prominent alumni throughout the world, who share how their HBCU experience molded them into the people they are today. We are also investing financially into HBCUs throughout the country. Our goal is to create a global movement of prominent HBCU alumni throughout the nation to continue to share their stories each year, allowing us to give back to prestigious HBCUs annually.

We are proud to present to you *The HBCU Experience: The HBCU Band Alumni Edition.* We would like to acknowledge and give special thanks to our amazing lead author/partner, Dr. Christy A.Walker, for your dedication and commitment. We appreciate you and thank you for your hard work and dedication on behalf of this project. We would also like to give a special thanks to our foreword author, expert authors, contributing authors and partners for believing in this movement and investing your time, and monetary donations, to give back to your school. We appreciate all of The HBCU Band Alumni who shared your HBCU experience in the FIRST EVER HBCU Band Alumni publication.

Dr. Ashley Little

About Dr. Ashley Little

Dr. Ashley Little is The CEO/Founder of Ashley Little Enterprises, LLC which encompasses her Media, Consulting Work, Writing, Ghost Writing, Book Publishing, Book Coaching, Project Management, Magazine, Public Relations & Marketing, and Empowerment Speaking. In addition, she is an Award-Winning Serial Entrepreneur, TV/Radio Host, International Speaker, Keynote Speaker, Media Maven, Journalist, Writer, Host, Philanthropist, Business Coach, Investor, Advisor for She Wins Society and 12X Best Selling Author. As seen on Black Enterprise, Sheen Magazine (Print and Online), Voyage ATL, Fox Soul TV, NBC, Fox, CBS, BlackNews.Com, Shoutout Miami, Shoutout Atlanta, TEDx Speaker, The Book of Sean, HBCU Times, VIP Global Magazine, The Black Report, Vocal, Medium, Hustle and Soul, BlackBusiness.com and many more.

She is a proud member of Delta Sigma Theta Sorority Incorporated, and a member of Alpha Phi Omega. She is very involved in her community, organizations and non-profits. Currently, she is the Co-Founder of Sweetheart Scholars Non-profit Organization 501 (C-3) along with three other powerful women. This scholarship is given out annually to African American Females from her hometown of Wadesboro, North Carolina who are attending college to help with their expenses. Dr. Little believes it takes a village to raise a child and to never forget where you come from. Dr. Little is a strong believer in giving back to her community. She believes our young ladies need vision, direction, and strong mentorship. She is the CEO/Founder/Visionary Author of The HBCU Experience Movement, LLC the first Black-owned company to launch books written and published by prominent alumni throughout the world who attended Historically Black Colleges & Universities. As authors, they share a powerful collection of stories on how their unique college experience has molded them into the people they are today. Our company's goal is to change the narrative by sharing Black stories and investing financially back into our HBCUs to increase young alumni giving and enrollment. Dr. Little is also the Editor and Chief of Creating Your Seat At The Table International Magazine, Advisor for She Wins Society, and Writing and Publishing Coach for the WILDE Winner's Circle.

She is the Founder and Owner of T.A.L.K Radio & TV Network, LLC. Airs in over 167 countries, streamed LIVE on Facebook, YouTube, Twitter and Periscope. Broadcasting and Media Production Company. This live entertainment platform is for new or existing radio shows, television shows, or other electronic media outlets, to air content from a centralized source. All news, information or music shared on this platform are solely the responsibility of the station/radio owner. She is also the Owner and Creator of Creative Broadcasting Radio Station the station of "unlimited possibilities" and Podcast, Radio/TV Host. She is also one of the hosts of the new TV Show Daytime Drama National Syndicated Television Show which will be aired on Comcast Channel 19 and ATT Channel 99 in 19 Middle Tennessee Counties. It will also air on The United Broadcasting Network, The Damascus Roads Broadcasting Network, and Roku. She is CEO/Founder/Visionary Author of The HBCU Experience Movement LLC and CEO/Founder of Little Publishing LLC.

Dr. Little is a 12X Best Selling Author of "Dear Fear, Volume 2 18 Powerful Lessons Of Living Your Best Life Outside Of Fear", "The Gyrlfriend Code Volume 1", "I Survived", "Girl Get Up, and Win", "Glambitious Guide to Being An Entrepreneur", The Price of Greatness, The Making Of A Successful Business Woman, and "Hello Queen". She is a Co-Host for The Tamie Collins Markee Radio Show, Award-Winning Entrepreneur, Reflection Contributor for the book "NC Girls Living In A Maryland World, Sales/Marketing/Contributing Writer/Event Correspondent for SwagHer Magazine, Contributing Writer for MizCEO Magazine,

Contributing Editor for SheIs Magazine, ContributingWriter National Sales Executive for Courageous Woman Magazine, Contributing Writer for Upwords International Magazine (India), Contributing Writer/Global Partner for Powerhouse Global International Magazine(London), Host of "Creating Your Seat At The Table", Host of "Authors On The Rise", Co-Host Glambitious Podcast, Partner/Visionary Author of The Gyrlfriend Code The Sorority Edition along with The Gyrlfriend Collective, LLC and CEO/Visionary Author of The HBCU Experience The North Carolina A&T State University Edition. She has been on many different Podcasts, TV Shows, Magazines, and Radio Shows. Lastly, she has received awards such as "Author Of The Month", The Executive Citation of Anne Arundel County, Maryland Award which was awarded by the County Executive Steuart L. Pittman, Top 28 Influential Business Pioneers for K.I.S.H Magazine Spring 2019 Edition. She has been featured in SwagHer Magazine, Power20Magazine Glambitious, Sheen Magazine, All About Inspire Magazine, Formidable Magazine, BRAG Magazine, Sheen Magazine, Front Cover of MizCEO Magazine November 2019, Front Cover for UpWords Magazine October 2019 Edition, Courageous Woman Magazine, Courageous Woman Special Speakers Edition November 2019, Influence Magazine, Featured/Interviewed On a National Syndicated Television Show HBCU 101 on Aspire TV, Dynasty of Dreamers K.I.S.H Magazine Spring 2019 Edition, Dynasty of Dreamers K.I.S.H Magazine September 2019 Edition, Front Cover of Courageous Magazine December 2019, Front Cover of Doz International Magazine January 2020, Top 28 Influential Business Pioneers for K.I.S.H Magazine, Power20 Magazine Glambitious January 2020, Power20 Magazine Glambitious February 2020, Featured in Powerhouse Global International London Magazine March 2020 edition, Featured in National Boss Magazine October 2020 Edition, Featured in Sheen Magazine February 2020 as one of "The Top 20 Women To Be On The Lookout For In 2020, BlackNews.com, BlackBusiness.com,

Front Cover She Speaks Magazine August 2020, Front Cover National Boss Magazine November 2020, BlackNewsScoop.com, Awarded National Women's Empowerment Ministry "Young, Gifted, & Black Award" February 2020 which honors and celebrate women in business such as Senior Level Executives, Entrepreneurs and CEO's below age 40 for their creativity and business development. Featured in National Women Empowerment Magazine 2020, Featured in Black Enterprise 2020, Featured on Fox, NBC, CBS 2020, Featured/Interviewed on National Syndicated Television The Black Report on Fox Soul TV, Front Cover for National Boss Magazine 2020, Speaker at The Black College Expo 2020, Speaker for Creative CEO's summit January 2021, International Speaker for Living Your Dream Life Summit 2021, Speaker for Elite Business Women Powershift Conference 2021, Keynote Speaker/Host/Panelist for The Bella, The Brand & Her Bag Wealth Summit 2021, Speaker for The Unstoppable You Summit January 2021, Speaker for Marketing Mastery Summit for Glambitious 2021, Speaker for Crown Yourself Conference January 2021, Featured in Sheen Print Magazine 2021, Speaker at Door Dash Virtual Black History Month Celebration, Speaker for Day Of Aggie Generations with North Carolina A&T State University, 2021 Woman of Black Excellence Honoree, Guest/Speaker on podcast The Happy Hour Show, Speaker for the Phoenix Jack & Jill HBCU Author Showcase, Guest/Speaker on The JMosley Show, Contributing Author for "Prayers For The Entrepreneurial Woman Book", Speaker for Creative Con, Recognized as one of Today's Black History Makers, Speaker at From Paper to Profits conference, Press Conference/Press for "Don't Waste Your Petty" Movie, Press Conference/Press for Mahalia Jackson movie, Speaker for HerStory Women's Global Empowerment Summit, Speaker for HerStory Women Who Lead Conference, Speaker for Stepping N2 Sisterhood Sharing Winning Secrets Virtual Summit, Speaker for I AM Glambitious Virtual Conference, Speaker for Black Authors Matter TV show, Speaker for Thought Leaders Global Virtual Summit, Speaker for A Conversation with Floyd Marshall Jr. as well to name a few.

Dr. Little received her undergraduate degree in English from North Carolina A&T State University. Next, she received her Master's Degree in Industrial Organizational Psychology. She has received her Doctorate in Humanitarian and Leadership as well. Dr. Little is a mover and shaker and she continuously pushes herself to be better than she was yesterday. She gives GOD all the credit for everything that has happened in her life. She has strong faith and determination to be great. She believes her only competition is herself. Her favorite scripture is Philippians 4:13 "I can do all things through Christ who strengthens me."

TABLE OF CONTENTS

Foreword
Ashley Maclin   3

Bandhead for Life
Dr. Christy A. Walker   11

Living Out My Legacy: Becoming a Legend
Dr. Kellye W. Hall, MD   19

They Call Me Mr. Drum Major Sir
Michael D. Lee   27

Marching to Preserve Our History: One Cadence at a Time
Desmond L. Kemp   35

An 80's Unconventional Journey to Sparta
John Newsome   43

Dreams Come True: How Mr. Walter F. Carlson Gave
Dr. Johnny B. Hodge, Jr. a Dream at N.C. A&T
Dr. John W. Hodge   49

THE BOX The Prairie View A&M University Drumline
PV McFunk Box 1987
SKIP Wilson   57

The Medicine of HBCU Band Participation
Dr. Kathryn D. Kelly, MD
Physician Owner, Kelly Collaborative Medicine   65

From the Band Room to the Boardroom

Deena Smith   73

Creations of a Bandhead

Gerard L. Howard   81

A Fixed Fight

Joseph Beard   89

The Reids Marching at "100" Percent Excellence:

A FAMU Rattler Story

Dr. Jorim & Aja Reid   95

Forever to Be a Mighty Marching Panther

LaToya Brooks   105

Who Would I Be Without the BGMM?

Ebony Burroughs   113

The Orange and Blue Crush, MSU

Dr. Bridgette Crawford Bell   121

From Band Camp to Hollywood: My'hBCU Band Experience

Davon Bagley   129

The Elite. The Untouchable. The Hampton University

Marching Force!

D. Rashad Watters   137

VSU Changed My Life & I'm So Glad

Taylor L. Whitehead   145

The Band Chose Me
Charles M. Conner   153

Band Changed My Life
Ernest Stackhouse   163

Perseverance, Accountability, Commitment, Dedication & Loyalty
Chase Arrington   171

Connection, Culture & Fellowship: My HBCU Marching
Band Experience
Herbert L. Seward III   181

The 101 Connection is Here… Shake Your Pluuuume! South
Carolina State University Marching 101
Jamie R. Brunson   187

The Defining Moment
David Matthews   195

A Casualty of Band Warfare
Derrick Black   201

Still Approaching: My Life & Times at Delaware State University
Chevis Anderson   207

The Machine that Saved My Life
Christopher Goins   215

A Whole New World
Keena Day   221

Don't Break Records: Set the Standard

Kelton J. Penson 229

When I Shed My Skin: A Rattler's Experience
in the Marching "100"

Stanley Holloway 237

Everlasting Influence

Stephen Edgerton 245

Bigger Than Band

Terri L. White 253

Stronger Than Adversity

Dr. Thomas L. Jones, Jr. 259

The Way of the 100

Tracey Jackson 267

Official Partners & Sponsors of the HBCU Experience
Movement, LLC 272

Ashley Maclin

Foreword
Ashley Maclin
Norfolk State University

One thing 2020 has brought is self-reflection.

Self-reflection on how far we, as people, have come. Individually, how have I grown? What do I still need to weather in order to grow? Most importantly, thank God I'm not where I used to be. This quarantine caused me to look back at what has helped shape and mold me into the person I am today. I'm a media personality, radio and television broadcasting talent, voice over talent and visionary. I'm heard throughout the Midwest, from Cincinnati to Columbus, Indianapolis to St. Louis. I've been featured worldwide in nationally syndicated morning shows, *Essence* magazine, Fox Soul and more. But my picture wouldn't be complete without my alma mater, my historically black college and university, Norfolk State University.

It was my senior year of high school. The year I was beyond ready to get out from under my parents' roof and start something new. From elementary school through high school, there was definitely structure. I had everything from music lessons, little league, soccer, marching band, tennis, swimming, chorus, fishing club, horseback riding, musicals and plays. Time management and pleasing other people were a few things I mastered at an early age. Higher education wasn't a suggestion or option either. It was my *next step* of what needed to happen. With this next chapter in my life, I wanted to make sure I was doing it for me.

My high school, Academies at Englewood, had guidance counselors help "guide" what colleges matched our interests. Interesting enough, these were mostly schools that didn't have my interests, nor people who looked like me. Mostly predominantly white institutions were suggested, so I began my own research. My grandparents are both graduates of HBCUs, my grandfather, a 1950 graduate of St. Paul's College in Lawrenceville, Virginia, and my grandmother, a 1951 graduate of Howard University. Their love for their institutions was invigorating and infectious. The stories, the love, the friends that turned into family... the pride. That was something I wanted to be a part of. Something I genuinely wanted to feel.

Toni Morrison said, "In this country, American means white. Everybody else has to hyphenate."

I have my whole life to be a "minority" by society's means. So, why not choose to go to an institution of higher learning—where I'm not a number—but a name with meaning and story. Others cared to help me define it. So, how did I get to Norfolk State? A friend of mine made a mistake.

While Hampton University was a possibility, one of the few people I knew who went to an HBCU suggested another school: North Carolina A&T. I never felt like I fit in with peers at home. My "friends" or people I associated with during that term didn't truly have the same interests or goals as me, except for a very select, hand-picked individuals. My friend, Keisha Thomas, who was currently attending A&T, where she marched for the Blue and Gold Marching Machine, was an exception. The one thing she shouldn't have done was show me a band battle between NCAT and Norfolk State from 2005!

I had *no* idea who this school was in green and gold! I had never heard of the school, but I was captivated by their discipline, their precision, their militant style, and how they commanded attention and respect. When I tell you Mr. Spartan and Captain Soul were *marching*. Speaking of marches, The Spartan Legion opened with the march "Malagueña" composed by Ernesto Lecuona. At that point, whatever little interest I had in the BGMM was depleted. I didn't know where Norfolk was, but by the end of this battle, it was clear to see who the better band was. Whoever the Spartan Legion was came to NCAT's gym and "stole their lunch" as my advisor and woodwind instructor, Stephanie Sanders, would say! Why did Keisha show me this battle? Let her tell it, she showed me this Band

Brawl DVD (no YouTube wasn't a thing) to get a taste of HBCU band culture. Even though she had a slight motive to get me to attend A&T, I knew the band experience I wanted to attend after watching. She had to be looking out for my best interests.

It was August of 2007 when my parents dropped me off for band camp. I did not know a soul. I was eager to leave from under my parents' roof and start something new. However, little did I know, I was walking toward a new family: The Spartan Legion, Sax Maniacs and Norfolk State University as a whole. I knew I was ready to get this "HBCU Experience" that my grandparents lived, breathed and always made sure to share stories about. The first story I was going to share is how I came to march alto sax. I was told, "No, you're going to play tenor. Your section leader is around the same height as you. You'll be fine."

This advice came from the best advisor, Stephanie Sanders. I'm barely 5' 2" and my instrument was just as tall as me. I didn't have much choice. I just accepted the challenge.

It was people like Stephanie Sanders, and the rest of our band staff, known as the "Dream Team" that helped shape my band experience and my growth through college. The team was led by our band director, Dr. O'Neill Sanford, who felt like a grandfather to every member in the program. He was tough, yet fair. He did everything he could to help his students. This was yet only another example of how I made the right choice by attending an HBCU. I can't speak for other institutions. But mine made sure to find a way to keep me enrolled in school. Mine continued to invest in me and my wellbeing. Norfolk State University has created in me a strong foundation that has been the basis of how I live my life today. From the strong friendships that have turned into family to the many lessons learned and the strong work ethic that has been bestowed in me, my HBCU paved a path for me. I have grown in ways that I could have never imagined possible if I went to a predominantly white institution. At Norfolk State University, we like to say, "Behold the green and gold." This comes from our university's theme song "Behold". This song strikes a chord that rings through the entire campus. It reminds you of something out of Medieval Times, where the horns ring the call and when the call is heard throughout the land. It's chilling. Hair raising. And you know The Spartan Legion is on the way. It's a spirit we carry as Spartans, and that spirit is enamored throughout my foundation. My band, my university, and my HBCU gave me the journey of a lifetime.

I wouldn't be the person I am today without the structure, work ethic, diligence, discipline and persistence the Spartan Legion provided for me. My love for music blossomed into a career. When I first began my radio journey, Norfolk State gave me the chance to learn even more at the school's radio station, HOT 91. The band had me host multiple band brawls. I hosted the BET College Tour when they came to NSU in 2012. I've traveled the world, performed at the *biggest* band showdown Honda BTOB, performing for President Barack Obama with the Spartan Legion. The list continues.

Similar to my story, many HBCU band alum feel just as strongly about their programs. This demonstrates love and compassion that you can only receive if you've marched in these prestigious bands. Nothing can replace such memories that we cling to so tightly. All HBCU band programs are fulfilling and enriched with legacy and honor. We will continue to honor such programs, invest in them and share our memories to continue to inspire the next generation to carry our torches.

P.S.

The Spartan Legion has the best version of "Neck". Not up for debate.

About Ashley Maclin

Ashmac is a radio personality with big goals and even a bigger personality that you can feel through the airwaves. Where listeners of Mac In The Midday are about to get real conversation that you have with your friends in a group chat, keeping you the know first of what's happening in the culture, and listening to your favorite tracks, with exclusives from your favorite artists. Get to know her even more on WHHL – HOT 104.1 and WHHH – HOT96.3 She is committed to sharing her platform for the greater good of others and serving the community. She is a member of Sigma Gamma Rho Sorority Inc., Tau Beta Sigma National Honorary Band Sorority Inc., and a proud HBCU graduate from Norfolk State University.

Her midday show from 10a-3p has captured listeners with quality content that is relevant to all ages, to timely conversations, and interviews that no one ever wants to miss. Ashmac has been featured in multiple markets from VA to Ohio as well as nationally. She's been featured on and through BET, ESSENCE, NBA ALLSTAR WEEKEND, media correspondent for FOX19, as well as Nationally Syndicated Rickey Smiley Morning Show.

Aside from her radio and media career, Mac is passionate about giving back to the community and institutions of higher learning. She supports many charitable programs and campaigns such as, but not limited to: Saving the Music, Feed The City Campaign, 1K Shoes for 1K Smiles, Toys for Tots, Stomp Out Hazing, NAACP's Bowl For Scholars, and The Urban League.

Ash continues to use her leadership and talent to make marks throughout the city as well as pursuing her career with nothing but passion. "I've always followed my love for music. Music is a universal language that everyone can understand without using one word. Music can bring out emotion from someone, make you reminisce, make you dance, make you cry, or make you turn up. I turn up every day and celebrate the fact I do something I love. Talk about music, your favorite artists, interview them, national news, local news, politics, entertainment, and more. That is a blessing." Interviews from Saweetie, Migos, T.I., Justine Skye, Danileigh, Moneybagg Yo, Mulatto, Angela Rye, and Corey Wise from *The Exonerated Five* are just a few names to mention. Her vibrant energy is something that is always felt, and energy doesn't lie.

Dr. Christy A. Walker

Bandhead for Life

Dr. Christy A. Walker

North Carolina A&T State University

I guess I was destined to be a member of an HBCU band. It's literally in my blood.

My earliest memory of seeing a HBCU marching band was when I was about four years old. Both of my parents were graduates of North Carolina A&T, where they met in the band. They were loyal alumni and attended A&T football games every season. When they brought me to games, I never paid attention to the football game itself, but the music always kept my attention.

I grew up in Hampton, Virginia, a city in close proximity to not one, but two HBCUs: Hampton Institute (now University), in Hampton, and Norfolk State University, which was thirty minutes away in Norfolk. I can recall attending Hampton football games at Armstrong Stadium with my grandmother when I was around five years old. Again, my eyes glazed over during the football game. However, I was always excited to see the band and the halftime show. I'll never forget those halftime band battles between Hampton and Norfolk State, known as the "Battle of the Bay", in the early 80's. Even as a five-year-old, I could tell that that band battle was intense! I knew that when I grew up, I would be in a band just like that.

I first met "Prof" Walter Carlson, A&T's band director when my parents marched, when I was six years old. He happened to be in town one day and stopped by our house to visit. Growing up, I always heard stories of how my parents marched at A&T under Prof. Carlson, how my dad was band president and trombone section leader, and how my mom was band secretary, a music major, and the only female member of A&T's brass ensemble.

By the time I reached high school, I knew I wanted to march at A&T. I had watched A&T's band every year for a decade. I knew I wanted to be there. Contrary to popular belief, my parents never forced me to go to A&T. They did, however, tell me they would pay for college if I attended an HBCU. It was *that* important to them. Regardless of influence, I had good grades, and I learned to play clarinet (my main instrument), flute, and piano. I was section leader in my high school band, and I played in all-city and regional bands.

I attended A&T's Visitors' Day for prospective students during my senior year, and met A&T's band director, Dr. Johnny B. Hodge, better known as "Doc", at the football game. I was nervous at first, but I walked up to Doc and introduced myself as Chauncey and Zenobia's daughter. He smiled, put his hand on my shoulder, pointed to the band and said, "Next year, you will be here." That was reassuring to hear.

The summer before my first band camp was a whirlwind. I was looking forward to marching in A&T's band, known as the "Blue and Gold Marching Machine". I knew there would be a big difference in my high school marching band experience and my college experience. My high school marched "corps style"—a roll step march with our feet close to the ground. I knew that A&T (and all other HBCU bands) primarily marched with a high-step style, which was much more physically demanding. I knew this would be a big adjustment, and I tried to get in physical shape ahead of time by running in my neighborhood in the combat boots I purchased for camp.

Our band camp schedule was as follows:
- 4:15 a.m. – Wake up (clothes were laid out the night before), shower, dress, walk to the practice field.
- 5 a.m. to 7 a.m. – Marching rehearsal
- 7 a.m. to– 9 a.m. – Breakfast and a quick nap
- 9 a.m. to 11 a.m. – Indoor music rehearsal
- 11 a.m. to 1 p.m. – Lunch
- 1 p.m. to 3 p.m. – Another music rehearsal

- 3 p.m. to 5 p.m. – Dinner
- 5 p.m. until – Outdoor rehearsal and sectionals

We did this all in the August heat. By September, I was in the best shape of my life.

I ended up marching for A&T all four years of college. We faced quite a few bands during those four years, but there are three memorable battles I would like to focus on:

The first collegiate game I played in was against Winston-Salem State University (WSSU) in September. I will always remember the exact day of this game because it was my eighteenth birthday! WSSU was only thirty minutes away from A&T and was historically one of A&T's biggest rivals. My mother grew up in Winston-Salem. Two of my aunts graduated from WSSU, and another aunt worked on the WSSU campus. That game was more than a rivalry – it was a family reunion.

Marching in that first game was intimidating. I knew the music, the formations and the dance routine. I had practiced it dozens of times, but it wasn't the same thing as actually performing it in front of a full crowd in Winston-Salem. All I kept thinking throughout the performance was, *Don't mess up! Don't forget to turn at the right time! Don't forget the dance routine and don't fall!* But all was well. The halftime show went on without issues.

The Winston-Salem game was also the first game where I faced an opposing band. I loved the feeling of literally facing your opponent and blowing songs in their direction. Then, of course, after the game, both bands played songs back and forth at each other, better known as a "5th Quarter".

The second game that was significant to me as a bandsman was the 1994 Circle City Classic in Indianapolis, when A&T played Southern University. Southern's band had a great reputation. I had grown up seeing their halftime show every year on NBC when they played Grambling State in the Bayou Classic. I was excited to see them face to face.

Southern's band had been known to intimidate other bands

due to their powerful sound and overall swagger. But they didn't intimidate us! I am glad that Doc taught us never to be intimidated by another band. That lesson sticks with me to this day. Back then, the Machine's nickname was the "Small Band with the Big Sound". We weren't really *that* small, but we were smaller than Southern's band. However, we didn't *sound* small. We ended up winning the Battle of the Bands that year. And, yes, we won because we received a trophy engraved with us as the winners, which is probably in A&T's band room somewhere.

The third game was when we played FAMU in 1996, my last year marching. It was significant because the band traveled to Tallahassee, Florida for the game. All of us recognized the history and legacy of Florida A&M's Marching 100. Bragg Stadium, FAMU's stadium, had a reputation of being tough to play in. FAMU's fan base is strong, and their fans are really passionate about their school. Not many bands traveled there.

Once again, the Blue and Gold Marching Machine was *not* intimidated by FAMU's band (or any others). Doc gave us the spirit of, "I'm not scared of anybody!", and it showed. We went in and played during the game and the halftime show, just as if we were in Aggie Stadium. At the end of the game, we filed out of our seats and walked across the field. We set up in concert formation in front of where FAMU was sitting. From there, our band and FAMU's band played songs back and forth during a "5th Quarter".

I don't remember who started it first, but both bands ended up playing some songs together. There was a rare spirit of camaraderie between the two HBCU bands. That night, FAMU's band threw a party and invited us. I still laugh about that party when I talk to people who were in FAMU's band back then.

When I think back to my time in the Blue and Gold Marching Machine, I have fond memories. I know people say that they met their best friends or their spouse through the band. People may be surprised, though, to find out that my best friends were not *necessarily* people I marched with in the band. Regardless, I still took away many lessons from the band. I learned musicianship, discipline, consistency, goal setting and, most importantly, confidence.

Now that I work as a college administrator, I have learned to appreciate the cultural significance of HBCU bands. I've learned to appreciate how they help in increasing student morale, refining campus culture, and bringing publicity to the university. They are the face of the university. They are the heart of HBCUs.

After college, I continued to keep up with HBCU band culture. In 1999, along with Michael Lee, I established an online community for HBCU bands called the 5th Quarter. Through The 5th Quarter, I have had the chance to mingle with people from just about every HBCU band. I've hosted gatherings, sat in luxury suites at stadiums, and even went on a cruise. However, I am proudest of the fact that, through my website, I was able to encourage students to march in an HBCU band.

The HBCU band family is a family. We have our quirks like any other family. But what I love the most is that I could meet anybody who marched in an HBCU band and have a common experience to talk about. It's been over 35 years since I started following HBCU bands. I used to think that I would *never* be that person in their 40s following HBCU bands. Now that I am in my 40s, I don't know what I was thinking back then. I have finally faced the fact that I'm gonna be a bandhead for life.

Lead Author Dr. Christy A. Walker

About Dr. Christy A. Walker

Dr. Christy A. Walker, is a higher education professional, bandhead, and HBCU advocate.

Christy, a native of Hampton, Virginia, earned a bachelor's degree in Chemical Engineering from North Carolina Agricultural and Technical State University (NC A&T). While Christy was a student at A&T, she played clarinet in the Blue and Gold Marching Machine and in the symphonic band for 4 years. This was a family tradition, as her parents met in A&T's band, and subsequently marched in A&T's alumni band for 40 consecutive years.

In 1999, Christy, along with Michael Lee, created The 5th Quarter, a website dedicated to showcasing HBCU marching bands. The 5th Quarter was considered a top resource for HBCU marching bands and received tens of thousands of unique visitors annually until its closing in 2019, after 20 years of service. The 5th Quarter has been profiled on the Huffington Post, and Christy has been interviewed on HBCU bands by the New York Times, CNN, the Associated Press, HBCU Digest, and the Charlotte Post. Christy has also written articles about HBCU bands for Halftime Magazine, created The 5th Quarter Podcast, and served as a regular panelist on the Marching Podcast.

Christy received a master's degree in Higher Education Administration from Old Dominion University and a doctorate in Higher Education Administration from Northeastern University. She currently serves at the Director of Career Services at Durham Technical Community College in Durham, North Carolina.

Christy is also the creator of the podcast, The HBCU Band Experience with Christy Walker, in which Christy interviews marching band alumni from different HBCUs. She is an Honorary member of Tau Beta Sigma National Honorary Band Sorority and a member of Sigma Alpha Iota International Music Fraternity.

Dr. Kellye W. Hall, MD

Living Out My Legacy: Becoming a Legend
Dr. Kellye W. Hall, MD
North Carolina A&T State University

Since elementary school, I knew I was going to be a member of the Blue and Gold Marching Machine. It was in my blood. My dad played saxophone in the band, while my Uncle Henry played trumpet. I began playing saxophone in the 6th grade. I could not wait to be in North Carolina Agricultural and Technical State University's (A&T) band. While I was always going to be an Aggie, I did have an appreciation for other Historically Black College and University (HBCU) bands.

I consider myself an honorary Floridian because my mom's side of the family is from Ft. Lauderdale. My aunt attended Florida Agricultural and Mechanical University (FAMU), so she was always touting the excellence of the Marching 100, the official name of the marching band. I was blessed to be able to attend the Florida Classic in grade school. This annual rivalry between FAMU and Bethune-Cookman College, now Bethune-Cookman University, allowed me to personally view the battle between two powerhouse bands. Bethune's Marching Wildcats were just as impressive to me as the Marching 100 and their "Let's Go Wildcats" song instantly had me dancing in my seat shouting, "WILD-CATS! LET'S GO-OOO!"

Over my childhood years, I observed numerous marching bands at A&T football games. I was mesmerized by the distinct personalities each had. Norfolk State's Spartan Legion immediately made me stand at attention, and I questioned whether I should salute as they marched by like Spartans ready for war. North Carolina Central University made their mark with their well-known chant, "N-C-C, NCCUUUUU!" Howard University's Ooh La La Dancers were sure to please. There were many more bands I did not get to observe in person, but I did see some in videos and on television.

Southern University's Human Jukebox is known for their undeniable brass sound, while Grambling State University's Tiger Marching Band stands out for the bass drum that is wheeled out in every performance. I could endlessly ramble about each HBCU band's signature style, but I digress. Don't get salty if I didn't mention your band. These are just my childhood memories.

The majesty that is HBCU Marching Bands is well-known, but the history may not be. The bands' stylistic approaches did not just emerge out of the sky, selectively inhabiting the spirits of black band members. Instead, it is reported the style all started with the military. In 1738, the Virginia Legislature required "free mulattos, blacks, and Native Americans to serve in the military."[1] However, they were not allowed to carry weapons due to fears of uprisings, so they served "as drummers, fifers, trumpeters, or pioneers."[2] Black men were recruited into military bands, and after the war of 1812, large numbers of all-black brass bands formed, particularly in New Orleans. Minstrel shows were popular in the late nineteenth century and early twentieth century, and black musicians came to the forefront in these shows at that time. Minstrel shows combined instrumental music, singing, dancing, comedy, acting, juggling, and other forms of entertainment. Initially performed by white performers in "black face," around 1840, black-owned minstrel troupes with all-black performers emerged.[3]

Minstrel shows became intermingled with brass bands and marching bands came about, particularly in New Orleans. They were not only a source of entertainment, but often a way to raise money for different organizations as well as bring awareness to these organizations,[4] which were important in the South, due to segregation.

Minstrel shows performed at night and to advertise for the shows, parades were held during the day. The drum major was the major attraction at that time, not unlike HBCU marching bands of today. The drum major was there to entertain, which included spinning a baton and dancing. The uniform of the drum major resembled a military band uniform but was altered slightly and included a tall plume on the hat or tails on the jacket, to distinguish him as the leader. A notable drum major is Bill "Bojangles" Robinson, also known as "Mr. Bojangles," the "King of Tap."[5]

In 1890, the first HBCU band at Tuskegee Normal School, now Tuskegee University was formed, directed by students. In 1907, the band had its first professional director, retired U.S. Army Major Nathaniel Clark Smith. The Marching 100 has been credited with the initiation of the modern-day style of high-stepping and incorporating dance moves into the shows. Dr. William P. Foster, the director at that time, forever changed the halftime show with this entertaining display and performance of upbeat styles of music, like ragtime and jazz.[6]

That's enough of a history lesson. Back to my story. I was fortunate enough to be exposed to HBCU bands early on, and once I was in high school, I was determined I was going to not only march in the Blue and Gold Marching Machine, but I was going to be drum major as well. I'll never forget seeing "The Machine" one particular Homecoming. The legendary drum major, Anthony Criss came onto the football field in a helicopter and the crowd's reaction to him creeping out of the helicopter solidified I was one day going to be the focus of the crowd's attention. Because I attended summer band camps for middle and high school students at A&T prior to my attendance there, I was able to interact with Anthony (Ant) and the band director at that time, Dr. Johnny B. Hodge. We were from neighboring counties, therefore, he affectionately nicknamed me, "Little girl from Warren County," which he continued to call me in college.

The band and Dr. Hodge were instrumental to me becoming the leader I am today. Doc, as we called him, was the reason I joined Tau Beta Sigma National Honorary Band Sorority, Incorporated (TBS). That was probably one of the best decisions I ever made. Those ladies not only groomed me to become more vocal, but I formed true bonds and friendships with chapter members that still exist today. If it were not for TBS, I may have never asked Dr. Hodge when we were going to get a female drum major, after I saw

South Carolina State University's marching band had one. I will never forget how quickly his laugh turned into the most serious demeanor when he said, "Never as long as I'm band director."

What I did not know was, A&T had never had a female drum major. As a matter of fact, female drum majors are unicorns in the HBCU Marching Band world, even today. Traditions die hard and females are certainly qualified to be drum majors, but the drum major is supposed to have a certain style and movement which is generally masculine. The next year, Doc changed his mind, and he chose me to be the first. You'll have to read that story in my memoir being released summer 2021. I would say, being chosen as drum major is still one of my greatest accomplishments to this day. I did not understand the gravity of the situation at the time, but unfortunately, there are still a lot of firsts women are accomplishing in not only HBCU bands but the world in general. FAMU just recently had their first female drum major selected in 2018, who is my sorority sister in TBS and Delta Sigma Theta Sorority, Incorporated. It is also rare that HBCU bands have female directors, something for my ladies to think about.

HBCU bands are paramount to many schools nationwide. They are used as a means of marketing for and recruitment of students to HBCUs. For many, the band is what drew them to the school. Oftentimes, people will tell you they come to the football games just to see the bands. This is best reflected at the beginning of the third quarter, when there appears to be a mass exodus of half the stadium that was full by halftime. As opposed to the clearing of the stands at Predominantly White Institutions (PWI) at halftime, stands at HBCUs are the fullest at halftime.

The "Fifth Quarter" is further evidence of the appeal for HBCU bands. While the football game may be over, the battle is just beginning for opposing marching bands. They play tunes back and forth while the dance squads battle for bragging rights. Marching band fans or "band heads" stick around to watch this clash until one band decides it is time to leave, either because they need to get on the road for a departure home or they ran out of quality songs to play. Regardless, it is an unofficial battle that HBCU bands take as seriously as the field shows.

Over the years, HBCU bands have become more popular and often imitated by high schools and PWIs because of the ingenuity and excitement brought to halftime shows. We have been the subjects of movies such as "Drumline" and Beyonce's "Coachella" performance used actual former HBCU marching band members to showcase elements of HBCU culture. For some, the band was something to do. For others, it was the only reason they even went to college. For me, it was a strong influence on the leader I am and a major reason I believe I made it into medical school. Every person has their own story, and the Blue and Gold Marching Machine was noteworthy in mine.

Expert Author Dr. Kellye W. Hall, MD

[1] Folkstreams. "A Brief History of African American Marching Bands." Accessed February 15, 2021. https://www.folkstreams.net/film-context.php?id.

[2] O'Bannon, Ricky. "Composers in Uniform." Boston Symphony Orchestra, June 22, 2016. https://www.bsomusic.org/stories/composers-in-uniform/.

[3] Clark, Robert H. "A Narrative History of African American Marching Bands: Toward A Historicultural Understanding." Journal of Historical Research in Music Education, May 6, 2019. https://doi.org/10.1177/1536600619847933.

[4] Folkstreams. "A Brief History of African American Marching Bands." Accessed February 15, 2021. https://www.folkstreams.net/film-context.php?id.

[5] Clark, Robert H. "A Narrative History of African American Marching Bands: Toward A Historicultural Understanding." Journal of Historical Research in Music Education, May 6, 2019. https://doi.org/10.1177/1536600619847933.

[6] Legacy History Pride. "HBCU Marching Bands." Accessed February 15, 2021. https://www.shoplhp.com/pages/hbcu-marching-bands

About Dr. Kellye W. Hall

Kellye Nichelle Worth Hall, MD does it all! A "Jill of all trades," early in life she was able to thrive in a variety of areas including academics, athletics, and the arts. She was always a natural dancer and even took tap and ballet classes as a child, but hip-hop was her passion. Growing up in rural Soul City, North Carolina, there were no hip-hop dance classes, so she and a group of friends came up with their own choreography, imitating popular artists of the time such as TLC.

Being a lover of music, she joined band and took up the saxophone as early as 6th grade. This led to her growing into a leader and eventually becoming drum major of her high school band. Being Aggie-born, she was destined to be a member of the Blue and Gold Marching Machine at North Carolina Agricultural and Technical State University, like her father and uncle. She was determined to lead the band as drum major and she achieved her goal, unknowingly becoming the first female drum major in the band's history in 1998. Due to the band's popularity, they became the official band of the Carolina Panthers, allowing Kellye to perform for crowds of over 70,000 people. She also joined the Theta Zeta Chapter of Tau Beta Sigma National Honorary Band Sorority, Incorporated and choreographed musical transitions for the step team in a number of step shows. As a senior, she was initiated in the Alpha Mu Chapter of Delta Sigma Theta Sorority, Incorporated. She is a Diamond Life Member and current member of the Charlotte Alumnae Chapter.

However, she knew from the age of two, her calling in life was to be a doctor. While she enjoyed dancing and performing in college, it was always only something to keep her busy while she was ultimately preparing to give her life to medicine. Her performing was halted, only to be revived yearly at A&T's homecoming, when alumni band members join the ranks with the University band to relive undergraduate days.

In 2018, she took her first hip-hop dance class at NC Dance District and instantly her passion for dance was renewed. After performing in Project: FULL OUT, the studio's seasonal performance concert, she was finally able to live the life of a dancer, even if it was only locally. Once Ana Ogbueze, the studio's founder, decided she wanted to pursue other projects, Kellye felt her purpose in life was shifting to serve people in a different way, through the art of dance. Though she spent most of her adult life as an Emergency Physician, she knew God was calling her to lead the studio. With Ana's mentoring and guidance, Kellye has taken a leap of faith that she can not only physically help people through medicine, but now she can spiritually and emotionally help people by encouraging them to grow as dancers and in life in general. Giving all glory to God, she knows how to bring out the best in people and she strives to continue the work Ana has started so people can live out whatever dreams they desire.

Dr. Hall is also a best-selling author, being one of the featured writers in the first edition of the HBCU Experience Anthology: The North Carolina A&T State University Edition. She is currently in the process of publishing her first memoir, to be released summer 2021. She intends to write future books, sharing different passions and life experiences. She gets enjoyment from mentoring young adults, more specifically, young black women that desire to become physicians, although she thrives off feeding into younger people no matter what direction in life they aim to take, hence her venturing into the field of memoir writing.

Kellye is a current resident of Charlotte, North Carolina and is a doctor, dancer, studio owner, mentor, author, and disciple of Jesus. She is married to her husband, Eric Hall, and mother to three dogs, also called her "fur babies."

Michael D. Lee

They Call Me Mr. Drum Major Sir

Michael D. Lee

Alabama A&M University

Being an HBCU marching band member has a way of humbling you. But it also builds you up to be a leader in life and professionally. Everyone, no matter your past marching experience, has to change in order to consume the culture and master your craft as a bandsman.

After seeing Alabama A&M play Central State University in the 1991 Circle City Classic, I knew for a fact that I wanted to be a part of a marching band program, especially after seeing the tall "lanky" drum majors from both schools. I remember that day like it was yesterday because it was an out-of-body experience.

During basketball season my senior year, I convinced my parents to allow me to take percussion lessons after practice twice a week. I was not in the band, so I worked on the weekends to afford to pay for the lessons. Every day after school and basketball practice, I practiced at home on a practice pad no less than two and a half hours per night.

After about four months of practice, I decided to audition for Central State University. I finished my high school years in Fairborn, Ohio, which was only about twenty minutes from Xenia, Ohio, where Central State was located. Early in the spring of 1992, I met Dr. James Oliver on the campus of Central State. He was one of the coolest band directors. Dr. Oliver auditioned me and ultimately gave me a pretty hefty marching band scholarship. He also helped arrange for me to get a Commuter's Grant, which paid my full tuition if I were to live off campus. The combination of these two financial aid resources essentially provided me with a full ride scholarship to Central State.

The stage was set. Mike Lee was going to be a Mighty Marching Marauder. However, around the time I was set to graduate, my dad, who was an Airforce Aviator for twenty-two years, decided to retire and move back to the city in which he went to college: Huntsville, Alabama. With my family moving to Alabama, my parents decided the risks were too great to allow me to stay off campus alone. So, I had to change my decision and attend Alabama A&M University in the fall.

I arrived on the campus of Alabama A&M University early in the summer of 1992, having been accepted just before graduation. I had a scheduled an audition with Mr. Arthur B. Wesley, the absolute best band director. Mr. Wesley allowed me to audition, and he gave me a scholarship. I'd auditioned for two top programs and achieved scholarships in both. Mike Lee was going to take over the world in the Alabama A&M University Marching Maroon and White Showband of the Sound! That hubris came to a screeching end the night of the band meeting on my first night on campus.

I Lost My Name

There was a lot I didn't expect when I arrived at the Morrison Building after walking from my dorm room at the top of the Hill (that is the nickname for AAMU's beautiful campus). The least of my expectations was the uncomfortable feeling I had walking into the auditorium.

After a few minutes, when everyone arrived, I saw upperclassmen hugging and laughing. Different groups were calling out sounds (sections have their own calls). I remember hearing Kappa Kappa Psi doing a call; it was utterly fascinating. It was hard to contain my excitement. However, it was important to remain cool, as if I had done this before. Just as I gathered my emotions, a loud, thunderous command came out of one of the three guys standing in front. Willie Lovejoy, the head drum major, called the band to attention. As the upperclassmen proceeded to call out in unison,

"One, two, three, four, five!" I sunk into my seat. I had no idea what was going on.

The meeting lasted about an hour. Mr. Wesley outlined what the camp schedule was and discussed many other topics. After the meeting, I decided to make my way out of the meeting after most of the upperclassmen had left. As I walked out, I saw a group of the percussion guys with S.T.I.X. on their shirts. As I walked past, an excited voice from the one and only Barney Smart caught me off guard.

He said, "What instrument do you play?"

I proudly exclaimed, "Snare drum."

Barney laughed like only he could and said, "You know what? Your name is Aya (pronounced Eye-Yah). That is what your name is!"

Ricky Williams, one of the percussion guys, immediately said, "Yes. His crab name is Aya." As I laid in my dorm room that night, I spend my last waking hours before band camp trying to figure out what a crab name was and why I got one.

Becoming Drum Major

At the end of my second year of marching as a bass drummer, my confidence had grown so much that I felt like I was a different person. I knew most people in the band, and I was being recognized on campus everywhere I went. Most people on campus called me by my crab name "Aya." Many of the marching band members remembered me when I would have to run to the middle of the field and yell, "I am Aya!" after practice while I was crabbing.

Being next in line to be the president of the Iota Nu Chapter of Kappa Kappa Psi, I had enough confidence now. I considered being a drum major and helping lead the band. I attended the mini drum major camp along with about ten other candidates. After the camp, the tryout stage was set. In the gym, the entire band sat on the bleachers close to the basketball court. One by one, each person trying out went through a preset routine in front of the band. Eventually, the bandmembers voted. That year, in 1994, there were two spots open. I won the first spot, and Jeremy Duncan (JD) won the second.

The first year, I learned what it meant to lead a program of that size. My second year, Shedrick and Chris (the two incumbent drum majors) finished, which made me the head drum major in 1995 and, subsequently, in 1996. During my time as head drum major, the band swelled to 310 members. I organized the drum majors as if they were vice presidents who were responsible for a certain number of sections. I oversaw the other drum majors and the auxiliary teams.

The band ran like a well-oiled machine and we outperformed any band that managed to challenge us. These were transitional years. We fine-tuned our marching style. The drum major's performance style changed with routines, and our drum major entrances became an entire performance in themselves. I earned the title "Mr. Drum Major Sir."

Life After Marching

Leaving a marching program can be traumatic. For the preceding four years (five years in my case), I had been a part of a cohesive family. We'd fought together, practiced together, cried, bled, grown and survived together. At the point of graduation, we were leaving it all behind. We realized then that there would never be a time when our family would fully be together again.

I graduated in 1997. One thing I desired to continue was the relationships I formed while I was marching. After speaking to Torey Jones, who I marched with both in the percussion section and as drum major, I got the idea of a website called The 5th Quarter. After purchasing the domain name, I received an email from Christy Walker, who asked about my plans were for the domain name. She purchased TheFifthQuarter.com, while my domain name was The5thQuarter.com.

Christy and I started the website in January of 1999, and it lasted twenty years. We were able to bring together many bandheads to one space, even before social media. Through that time, I grew in my career. The culture of marching band continued to grow through the website. Leading the effort, I was able to grow in the IT field and programming.

Marching band gave me the opportunity to develop my skills and leadership abilities by simply welcoming me into the culture. Through my years at Alabama A&M, I was able to grow into myself. I developed a strong sense of purpose and belonging. I was able to nurture my desire to lead. I networked. I learned about deep binding friendships and trust. These skills have propelled me to lead large groups in corporate America. I ran for public office and won two terms on the Durham Public Schools Board of Education. I am a senior leader in the Customer Success Industry. I owe everything I am to the bonds and experience I received in the HBCU marching band program.

I would do it all over again, if given the chance.

Expert Author Michael D. Lee

About Michael D. Lee

Mike Lee is a proud graduate of Alabama A&M University in Normal, Alabama where he marched for five years in the Marching Maroon and White Showband of the South. Mike played bass drum for two years and was a drum major for three years, two of which he was the Head Drum Major. While Mike was head drum major, the Marching Maroon and White band reached numbers just over three hundred.

During his time at AAMU, Mike majored in Computer Science with a Minor in Mathematics. Currently, Mike is the Director of Customer Success at Spreedly, a Software as a Service payment orchestration leader. He leads a team of Customer Success Professionals focused on value driven relationship building as well as churn prevention, application adoption planning, and subscription renewal engagements.

After his graduation from Alabama A&M University, Mike started his career as a Java Developer. He quickly moved up to various leadership roles and explored other aspects of technology including Systems Engineering, Database Engineering, and Network Engineering. During this time, he co-created the HBCU Marching Band website The 5th Quarter (www.the5thquarter.com) which lived for 20 years working to preserve the craft of HBCU Marching Band.

In 2011 Mike completed his MBA at the University of Massachusetts at Amherst with a focus on Information Technology Management and Strategic Planning. After his MBA degree was completed, Mike moved into Program, Project, and Product Management at Credit Suisse. After 17 years in the IT industry, Mike was introduced to Customer Success at Apptio, Inc, and found that the experience in his background prepared him to grow rapidly within this space.

Currently Mike is a Doctoral Student and the University of North Carolina at Charlotte where he plans to focus his DBA research on how mid to large companies can measurement and predict the continuous loss of value in software as a service products and services as it relates to renewals and churn.

Mike holds certifications: PMP, CSM, QTC, Greenbelt, PSM I to name a few.

Mike is a husband and father of three children Nicholas, Peyton, and Cameron and a member of the Durham Public Schools Board of Education where he was Chairman for 4 years. Mike also sits on various boards and committees for the county of Durham and North Carolina.

Mike believes that his time as a member of the Alabama A&M University Marching Maroon and White, prepared him to succeed in life by teaching him leadership, confidence, determination to succeed despite the challenges that lay in front of his path.

Desmond L. Kemp

Marching to Preserve Our History: One Cadence at a Time

Desmond L. Kemp

North Carolina A&T State University

Marching band has been my first love since I was two years old. If you glance through the photo album of my toddler years, you will see various pictures of me sitting in the grass with a Flocked Aussie hat covering my head. It just so happened that Aussie hat was worn by the band at my high school during the 1980s. In 1984, my aunt Adriene was appointed the first Black female drum major at Hoke County High School. I've been told that whenever she would lead the band onto the field, I would stand up, mimic her commands, and direct the band along with her. That was only the beginning.

After graduating from high school, she went on to attend Fayetteville State University and marched with the Marching Bronco Express. For years, we spent our fall Saturdays at Fayetteville State football games. I always looked forward to hearing the drum tap and drum major's whistle striking up the band as they chanted, "F- S- U!" It was something about the movements of FSU's band that made me memorize each step. After each game, I found enjoyment practicing those moves in the front yard. I had toy instruments, flags, batons, and my hat. I acted out the role of every band unit for hours. I grew very fond of the saxophone and flag sections.

Most true 'bandheads' know about the BET Bandfest of 1986. I was merely only four years old when this special aired on television. My mom recorded it for me. For the next two years, I played the tape while marching, dancing and chanting as each band would do during the breakdown. My cousin Ebony (Ladysticks) would sometimes be alongside, memorizing drum cadences. We found ourselves twelve years later marching in our high school's band. I believe our early exposure to the musicality of Black college bands inspired us to be musicians.

Prior to the 2010s, The Marching Bucks at Hoke High was a corps-style band. I was appointed to the role of band captain my senior year. I was very enthused about the leadership position and I spent a lot of time digging through the crates for music for us to play during football and basketball games. I landed on three arrangements by Mr. Warren Shaw: *Get Ready, Never Satisfied,* and *Before I Let Go.* In pure excitement, I quickly scurried across the band room to grab my saxophone to begin memorizing the arrangements. As I started to play, my classmate, O'Neil, came in with his trumpet and we jammed. After a few rehearsals, we ended up convincing our band director to let us play *Before I Let Go* and *Get Ready* that season.

I spent a lot of time talking with my cousins, Karen and Mary Patricia, that year. Both of them are Aggies and band alumni. Karen schooled me on the fact that the flag line was called The Untouchables, which she was a member of. Mary Patricia marched in the band in the 1960s. I visited her classroom and we'd somehow always end up talking about band. I can still hear her saying, "My best memories of A&T are in the band, and I learned how to move!" Mary Patricia is now deceased. But I'm sure if she was reading this, she would probably show everybody that she still had those moves.

O'Neil and I found ourselves in the ranks of the Blue and Gold Marching Machine in the fall of 2001. Attending North Carolina A&T was already a big deal. But marching in the band made it worthwhile. I gained some of the greatest friends from the band. My best friend Kiera and I marched on the same squad during my freshman year. It's funny that our friendship started with her sitting in my assigned seat. I asked her to move so I wouldn't have to run laps. She slid over as I attempted to ask her if she was a freshman, as well. She frowned at me and let me know she was an upperclassman. She says our friendship started because I talked to her first. I digressed; the cat has been let out of the bag in this book.

Every time we lined up to parade through campus to the stadium, I got an adrenaline rush as the drum majors would call off,

"Whistle, two, three, four!" As soon as we responded with "Up, two, out, up," I lost all feeling in my legs. Marching down the hill, swinging my sax left to right, and chanting, "Uh ohhhhhhhhh…uh ohhhhhh" was exhilarating. My friends always told me they heard our band approaching in their dorm rooms across campus. Many people ran out to the strip to watch because they knew the Blue and Gold Marching Machine was coming in full force.

I lived in the moment. As a freshman in the band, in general, your thoughts are to be present for every performance and rehearsal because you might get cut. It just so happened that we were asked to perform during a pep rally and another event during classes. I felt like I had to be there. Both performances cut out the instructional time in my English Literature course. My English professor, Dr. Taylor, was a proud "alumnae of Ayantee," as she would state. She honored being an Aggie and expected her students to respect the legacy of our institution.

There were two other band students enrolled in this course. Before the second performance, neither of them came to class. I informed Dr. Taylor that I would be leaving after thirty minutes so I could make it to the band room on time. She confirmed that it would be my second time leaving her course, but she made sure that I asked a peer to share their notes with me after leaving.

I said, "No problem!"

Time rolled past and she noticed that I was packing to exit. I proceeded to walk out then she stopped me.

"Mr. Band… if you leave my class again after today, you're going to have to get your degree in band. I'm not excusing you again. No more leaving my class. I will see you when you march by."

My whole class laughed as I walked out. I shamefully walked to the band room and told Dr. Hodge what she'd said. Dr. Hodge looked at me and laughed.

"Well, boy, you are a college student first. I know you have class." His delivery was witty and apparent that the expectation was for me to handle my business as a student first.

Each lesson instilled by Dr. Johnny B. Hodge and Dr. Kenneth Ruff shaped my ability to perform in the workplace. Marching in a Black college band imparted the value of *loyalty*, practice and discipline. If I hadn't learned those values in the Blue and Gold Marching Machine, I would not have seen the accomplishments I have since graduating.

I've had the pleasure of attending many HBCU football games and Battle of the Bands. Regardless of the conference, every former band member I've met will tell you their band is the best. Although, Southern's Human Jukebox seemed to not let us forget that *U.S.A. Today* coined them the baddest band in the land. I realize for some of us, marching band was a safe haven. It was an escape from our worries and the comfort needed in sorrowful times. But at an HBCU game, the band is the heartbeat of the experience.

Today, marching bands are a major attraction for HBCUs. Some people praise the movie *Drumline* for the following. But honestly, HBCU bands have been appealing since Dr. William P. Foster began designing innovative drills and incorporating the high-stepping style for the Marching 100 at Florida A&M University in the early 1900s. When I mentioned the idea of this book to the HBCU Experience, I hoped to begin the trend of preserving the history of Black college bands. To find out this book was in the works, I was excited to join the team to develop this project. Stories of prominent Black college alumni, like Ronald McNair, participating in the band and fraternal organizations tend to be excluded from historical texts. Each library on every college campus should have a marching band archive, but there are only a few. It is our duty as HBCU alumni to preserve the true legacy of Black colleges and their elements.

I appreciate Dr. Ashley Little and the HBCU Experience team for providing a platform for Black college band alumni. Because of my love for band, I began to reach out to some of my favorite bandsmen to tell their stories. Dr. Christy Walker, the founder of the Fifth Quarter Band Forum was the first. There was no way I wanted this book to be released on HBCU bands without talking about The Fifth. That forum introduced me to my best friends, Helena and Chuck 'Piccolo' and many others who love the band as much as I do.

The shared memories in this book are only a snippet of an HBCU bandsman's experience. It's beyond the jig you watched us do on the field. Many tears were shed by some who only had the band to keep them from dropping out of school while the college transition made them homesick. Some of us traveled out of state for the first time in the band.

A few of us met our first love in the band.

But all of us marched *for the love of the band.*

Expert Author Desmond L. Kemp

About Desmond L. Kemp

Desmond L. Kemp is an American Studies Ph.D. student at Indiana University Purdue University- Indianapolis, writer, activist, and accomplished educator. As a civics, college and job readiness instructor in Chicago, Kemp managed to collectively guide his students in achieving over $8 million dollars in scholarships. He is a proud alumnus of North Carolina Agricultural and Technical State University. Prior to attending graduate school, he served as an AmeriCorps VISTA. He completed his masters at DePaul University in the Master Applied Professional Studies with minor studies in Educating Adults.

In 2015, he released the first book of the teen fiction series, Uncommonly Common. He is also a contributing author for the HBCU Experience: North Carolina A&T Second Edition. Desmond is a member of Phi Beta Sigma Fraternity, Inc. and the National Forum for Black Public Administrators. Desmond's favorite hobby is working as a stand-in and featured model on some of your favorite television dramas.

John Newsome

An 80's Unconventional Journey to Sparta

John Newsome

Norfolk State University

To accurately capture my decision to attend Norfolk State University to further my education, and join the "Marching Spartan Legion", you have to take a journey back in the time machine to circa 1982 when I was a freshman in high school. It was at that time that I began to foster a love for the HBCU band culture. My high school band director was a FAMU graduate, former member of the famed "Marching 100" and former section leader of the "White Whales" Sousaphone section. Because of him, I was exposed to some of the finest HBCU bands in the country, like, Southern University, Tennessee State University and Grambling State University, to name a few. Growing up in this era, who didn't watch with admiration the Coca-Cola commercial that featured Grambling's "World Famed" marching band?

I had my heart set on attending Florida A&M University in 1985. After earning a music scholarship, it wasn't much that could deter me from what I thought was an inevitable next step in my academic and musical journey. That was until one fateful evening when my cousin Doris Mangrum came to Atlanta with a few of her friends and former Norfolk State University professors to attend a teachers' convention. My cousin Doris was a legend in her own right. She is a Hampton University graduate, a former Norfolk State University professor and a women's basketball coach. Doris is also an inductee in the Norfolk State University sports hall of fame and the CIAA sports hall of fame. She and her friends stopped by my grandmother's house to visit, and I was summoned to the dinner table to have a discussion. In some ways, it felt more like an intervention!

Doris knew that I was set on attending FAMU. After convincing my older sister, Carla Newsome-McManus, to change her course of direction to attend Norfolk State University on a Mathematics and Computer Science scholarship, I got the sense that Doris felt her work was undone. She was determined to secure the package deal of getting both me and my sister to Hampton Roads. When describing the Norfolk State University marching band, she simply said, "We don't call our band just a marching band. We call them the legion!" For whatever reason, those words resonated with me enough to warrant further investigation. Doris began the process of getting me in touch with the Norfolk State University Director of Bands. I would venture to guess that she projected a sense of urgency as I was contacted by NSU's Director of Bands a couple days later.

The Norfolk State University Director of Bands at the time was Mr. Emery L. Fears. Mr. Fears has been credited with creating the concept of the "Spartan Legion" back in the early 70s. He is widely considered a legend in the music community. He is a Tuskegee University graduate, as well as a University of Michigan graduate. He served as Director of Bands at I. C. Norcom High School and Manor High School before taking the helm at NSU. He led his high school bands to eighteen consecutive number one ratings in musical festivals, playing the most complex classification of music for high schools at the time. At the time I was considering NSU, Mr. Fears was one of only two African American bandmasters to be inducted into the National Bandmasters Association. The other notable name is William P. Foster, former Director of Bands at Florida A&M University. Needless to say, Mr. Fears had an impressive list of credentials and accomplishments that I had no clue about until I began my recruitment process with NSU.

But, still, the question remained. Is this band any good?

My initial conversation with Mr. Fears was one of the most engaging and enlightening conversations a young man could ever have. His knowledge of music and marching bands outside of the one he was tasked with leading was quite impressive. Mr. Fears did not deliver the "hard sell" to me. He was more concerned with making sure the music program and the university overall were a good fit for me. After a few follow-up conversations with Mr. Fears, I felt comfortable enough to flip my decision to attend NSU, knowing I would have a family support system in the area to help guide me along my collegiate journey. In fact, I felt so comfortable that I convinced my best friend Roger Brathwaite to join me. Roger later became assistant section leader of the Dizziacs trumpet section. We both joined by faith, hoping that we were joining a great marching band, even though the Norfolk State University's "Marching Spartan Legion" was "sight unseen" to us. A risky proposition, that's for sure!

In the late summer of 1985, or in other words, "the point of no return", I found myself excited about band camp and the freshman intake process. But that excitement was tapered by a bit of apprehension. Had I made the right decision? Well, it was too late to worry about that. I'd arrived on campus. I was simply ready to meet my fellow freshman colleagues and get to work!

The first day of band camp was an eye-opening experience for me. I found that work was intense and rigorous, and the expectations were high. The biggest takeaway for me initially was a caliber of musicians in the incoming freshman class. In a class of 70+ freshmen, the level of musical aptitude left me feeling inadequate, which is exactly what I needed! Honestly, if I had any inclination that I was the best musician in the room, there was probably not much for me to aspire to become. I needed peers who were musically better than me to elevate my level of musicianship.

Still sight unseen, I was anxious to get a taste of what "The Legion" looked like in action. A sample of what I could expect to experience between the lines on the football field at halftime, a video viewing session one evening during band camp afforded me that opportunity. Queued up was the 1984 halftime performance of the NSU vs. Hampton University game at Armstrong Field in Hampton, Virginia. If I could describe it in one word, it would simply be *wow*! The Legion put on an up-tempo, intense and exciting halftime show that seemed to do nothing short of leaving smoke on the field! The dance routine was like nothing I had ever seen before, with the band split into four blocks and each block doing an individual mini dance routine to an up-tempo drum break. It was capped off with a pop-lock routine on the fifty-yard line, performed by Dexter "D'Extra" Wiley, former member of the MDFS percussion section and member of the 90s new jack swing R&B group, II D Extreme. From the opening fanfare of "Toccata and fugue in d minor" to the field exit to "I'm So Glad", it was entertaining. It was at this point that I knew I had made the right decision!

I often reflect on the time spent at Norfolk State University and being part of what is now regarded as one of the premier HBCU bands in the country. I wonder, if given the opportunity to do it all over again, if I would have chosen NSU. I can say, with absolute certainty, yes, I would! The experience I gained was invaluable. The friendships I made are lifelong. I learned patience, perseverance and leadership. Above all, I learned to be accountable for which direction my life would go. Nothing is given to you. Everything has to be truly earned! This is what I learned while attending NSU. Sure, these life lessons could have been acquired at other prestigious HBCUs. But, for me, NSU was a perfect fit. I will forever bleed green and gold and shout the NSU battle cry.

"Behold the green and gold!"

About John Newsome

John is a 1989 graduate of Norfolk State University and a proud alumnus of the "Marching Spartan Legion" where he served as section leader of the "Dehoinz" Mellophone section. John pledged Alpha Phi Alpha Fraternity, Inc. Epsilon Pi chapter at Norfolk State University and earned a B.S. Degree in Electronics Engineering Technology.

John has worked in the field of Cyber-Security for over 20 years and presently works as a Technical Solutions Architect for Cisco Systems. John has been married to Aprile Newsome (a graduate of Hampton University) for 27 years and together they have three children (Teylor 26, Sydnee 19 and Giovanni 15.) John is a native of Atlanta, GA and presently resides in Snellville, GA.

Dr. John W. Hodge

Dreams Come True:
How Mr. Walter F. Carlson Gave
Dr. Johnny B. Hodge, Jr. a Dream at N.C. A&T

Dr. John W. Hodge

North Carolina A&T State University

Decades of sacrifice, hundreds of football games, thousands of students, and millions of fans are tough to grasp for any reader. However, those familiar with the world of HBCU bands will find my words familiar. Hopefully, this makes sense to the fans who cheer for our teams and scream for our bands every Saturday. This is written with you in mind.

There were several brilliant band directors, like Jimmie J. Williams and Howard T. Pearsall, who made significant contributions to the marching band at A&T. It would be impossible to name them all. However, few have held the title of Director of Bands for Eighteen years or more. This group is one of A&T's most exclusive. It includes Mr. Walter F. Carlson, Dr. Johnny B. Hodge and Dr. Kenneth G. Ruff. All three men have placed their special signatures on the Blue and Gold Marching Machine that can be seen even today by those with discerning eyes for marching bands. In my humble opinion, the road to the famous *Aggie band we saw during the tenure of the Hodge years* began way back in 1955, during a chance meeting between Walter Carlson and sixteen-year-old Johnny B. Hodge. Back in those days, A&T was a marching band mecca. High school band directors brought their ensembles from throughout the state, with the hope of showing their mastery of music and superiority over other high schools. Henderson Institute of Henderson, North Carolina was one of many such bands. On this particular day, their goal was to show all other bands, even the famed Dudley High School Marching Panthers of Greensboro, that Henderson Institute was the real deal.

As young Johnny B. Hodge and his best friend, Kemp Talley walked onto campus, they were mesmerized by its size. Imagine, all of these buildings were built to educate what were then called *colored* people. The professors in these buildings were also *colored.* Those thoughts alone were enough to overwhelm a sixteen-year-old mind. However, a pivotal moment happened in the life of Johnny B. Hodge, Jr. that day. As he and Kemp made their way across campus, they saw *him.* The distinguished Navy veteran, member of the world-famous United States All-Negro Navy Band, and the then current band director of the renowned, distinguished, world-class marching band of "Ayantee." Walter F. Carlson was a giant in the world of music. And there he was, standing right in front of Johnny and Kemp.

The way the story was told to me, Kemp dared Johnny to say something to Mr. Carlson. If you knew Johnny B. Hodge, Jr., you would *know* that a dare was something he unlikely turned down, especially one like this. So, Kemp and Johnny walked toward the man they believed was the king of marching bands. All of the sudden, Mr. Carlson stopped what he was doing and noticed the two awkward teens, who were literally shaking in their shoes. After Kemp's dare, what would Johnny say? Hello? I like your band? No. Johnny B. Hodge, on that day in 1955, shared his ultimate dream.

He said, "I want to work for you one day, Mr. Carlson." And to his credit, instead of killing the dream of a teenager, Mr. Carlson added fuel to the fire inside him.

He replied, "If you keep working hard, you'll get here." That was all Johnny needed to hear. How many times did Johnny's future students hear words about the importance of hard work? Like Johnny on that day in 1955, many of them listened.

So, Kemp and Johnny jogged away to finally get with their Henderson Institute band. As they jogged, Johnny asked Kemp a question.

"So, Kemp, what do you want to be?"

Kemp stopped jogging, pointed up into the air and said, "I want to fly, Johnny, just like the Tuskegee Airmen."

Just so you know how much Mr. Carlson's words meant to Johnny, he thought his dream was bigger than Kemp's.

As time passed, Johnny headed to North Carolina Central, and Kemp actually attended "Ayantee" where he played under the baton of the great Walter Carlson. Johnny and Kemp stayed in touch as best they could, but this was before email and social media. Both men graduated from college, began careers and started families.

Years later, in 1972 Johnny and the love of his life, Brenda Bethel Hodge, attended a conference for music educators. Brenda enjoyed the city. She attended a few conference sessions with Johnny. The *secret* many NCCU Eagles knew that few Aggies ever realized was that Johnny's wife, my mom Brenda, was the superior musician. She was a child prodigy at piano who played some of Sergei Rachmaninoff's most complex compositions when she was only 15-years old.

While at the conference, the same thing that happened in 1955 happened again. Johnny saw Walter Carlson. As if the conversation that had started in 1955 continued, Walter F. Carlson offered Johnny B. Hodge, Jr. a job.

He said, "I've been watching you. Richard Jones, Clarke Edgerton, J.Y. Bell and I think you might be the right one. How would you like to work for me?"

The thirty-three-year-old Johnny could hardly speak. He was overwhelmed. His answer was awkward, but true.

"I've been dreaming about that since high school."

So, here we are. We've spanned the years from 1955 to 1972. Johnny and Kemp meet Walter Carlson in 1955. Johnny hoped to be a band director with Mr. Carlson and Kemp Talley hoped to be a pilot. Johnny and his wife Brenda had just attended a music educators' conference where Walter Carlson offered Johnny a job.

I need you to know something, and I want you to know it without question. When God has a plan for your life, it reads like a story. This is so because God is the *author* and the *finisher* of our faith. If you think I'm a preacher trying to convince you, please stop wasting time. I'm a sinner who writes. But whether you believe or not, I have no doubt that *you* have a divine purpose for your life. I encourage you to find it.

Johnny and Brenda got on an airplane back to Greensboro from the conference. The most amazing aspect of the trip to them at the time was that *colored people* could now fly on airplanes with white folk, which was a step toward real progress.

As the flight began, a voice of someone who sounded familiar to Johnny became audible.

"Good afternoon ladies and gentlemen. It is my honor to fly you safely home. Joining me to make your flight as safe and comfortable as possible is a dedicated team of professionals. And before I forget, this is your captain speaking, Kemp Talley."

Kemp indeed became one of the first black men to fly for a commercial airline, just as he had always dreamed. On one of his thousands of flights, he flew his childhood friend, Johnny, back home to Greensboro, where Johnny began his journey with North Carolina A&T State University as a band director.

In 1991, I called my dad about band camp. I was at my first Army duty station in Fort Ord, California. Dad said, "Our numbers are low, but these kids can play their butts off. We've got a big contest coming up in Atlanta. There will be bands from all over the country with numbers as high as 300."

I asked, "How many kids do you have, Dad?"

He replied, "Oh, by the end of band camp, I'll have a *Block 96*, and we are going to win this damn thing."

Trust me. There was absolutely no doubt in his voice.

Of course, I didn't believe him until he called me back weeks later.

He said, "We won *Best All-Round Band* with 96 kids. Told you so!"

That's another thing about the great Dr. Johnny B. Hodge, Jr. When he was right, he reminded you. But pause right now and realize that Johnny's journey to that historic victory began thirty-six years earlier, when he was just a teenager. Instead of killing his dream, Walter Carlson *fueled* it. This is something we should all do for young people.

And, as if God were writing a movie script, one day, Dr. Johnny B. Hodge, Jr. met a teenager named Kenneth G. Ruff who is now Dr. Kenneth G. Ruff.

Many years later, Dr. Ruff became the Director of Bands at North Carolina A&T State University. Amen.

About Dr. John W. Hodge

Dr. John W. Hodge is president and co-founder of Urban Learning and Leadership Center (ULLC), an organization focused on student achievement and reduction of the achievement gap. He has served as a reading teacher, English teacher, AVID teacher, Assistant Principal and Associate Director of AVID Center Eastern Division. AVID (Advancement Via Individual Determination) is an international college-prep program. He served as Director of An Achievable Dream Academy, an inner city school that piloted many of the interventions used by Urban Learning and Leadership Center. An Achievable Dream Academy is a high performing, high poverty school that has received numerous national awards.

John received his Bachelor of Science degree from North Carolina A&T State University where he graduated with honors. He later received his Master of Arts degree from Chapman University. John completed his academic and professional preparation by earning a Doctor of Education degree from Virginia Tech where he conducted extensive research on factors that contribute to the academic success and/or failure of impoverished children.

What sets Dr. John W. Hodge apart in the field of education is his well-documented ability to put research and theory into everyday practice in rural, urban and suburban schools. Dr. Hodge has helped educators in elementary, middle and high schools make the necessary changes to help all children meet and exceed rigorous academic standards. He is known as a master teacher and staff developer.

Dr. Hodge's career has been defined by assisting students and teachers overcome obstacles and achieve goals. He has also served as an inspirational speaker throughout the United States.

Dr. John W. Hodge is truly one of America's most respected new voices in education. His presentations are often "the spark" for schools in their quest to meet and exceed state/federal accreditation standards and implement strategies for continuous improvement. Dr. Hodge is an expert in helping schools create and sustain academic excellence.

Prior to starting his career in education, Dr. Hodge distinguished himself in the service of our country with the 7th Infantry Division of the United States Army.

SKIP Wilson

THE BOX
The Prairie View A&M University Drumline PV McFunk Box 1987

SKIP Wilson

Prairie View A&M University

When I hear our moniker chant, B..O..B..O…X…X., it always sends a chill down my spine. It's not an awkward chill, but a chill of pride. Sometimes it's overwhelming but it happens every time. When greeting one of my BOXBROTHERS or BOXSISTERS, answering the phone, hanging up the phone, thanking them, congratulating them, consoling them in times of pain, or whatever the situation calls for, we always say, B.O. Its nuts, but it's us.

> The phone will ring, (ring, ring),
> Me: Hello
> BOXBROTHER/BOXSISTER: What's up B.O.?
> Me: What's up B.O.?

It's funny that I just had that "chill" just typing that interaction, LOL… but it is what it is. We are a self-contained unit and we all have our personal and different lives but we always circle back to each other for advice, comradery, help and networking. I genuinely love these people and hopefully they love me back, because we are a Fraternity of Souls. We never seem to run out of stories because we all experienced the BOX differently but at the same time, we all experienced the BOX the same way. I said that to say that our Brotherhood is unmatched and unwavering and we wouldn't have it any other way.

My journey with the PV McFunk BOX started totally by accident. I never had any intentions of actually attending Prairie View A&M University, I in fact, was one hundred percent going to become a Texas Southern University Tiger. I was raised on the Ocean of Soul and the "Funk Train", which is the drumline at TSU.

One day, I went to the Texas Southern vs Southern University game, it's 1984, I'm in the 10th grade, going to my first HBCU game. We actually went to see Third LeBlanc in Southern University's drumline, the Funk Factory, he was from my high school, and his dad was my band director, Mr. Sylvester Leblanc. But anyway, TSU was lined up in the endzone, then the drum major blew the whistle, the band played "Talking out the side of Yo Neck", while slow marching out of the endzone, let's just say I was hooked.

For the next three years, I was one hundred percent TSU. Then one day, a friend of mine, Kerry Norton, asked me to ride with him from Houston, Texas to Prairie View A&M University, Texas (LOL); because back then, Prairie View was wayyyyyyy in the country, but Kerry needed to go audition for the Man, the Myth, the great, Professor George "Prof Ed" Edwards. Kerry was a sax man. So while he was auditioning, I was hanging out in the band room, that's when I met a few BOX cats. They were standing over by the drums talking and I was just looking around, and I saw a tenor drum with heads on both sides, which was crazy to me because PV marched downright tenor drums at the time. I asked them if I could swing on a drum, and one of them said, "what's up, are you crabbing?" I said, "nawl, I'm going to see you boys from across the field, I'm going to the funk train." We laughed, and they actually let me play on the drum. Let me tell y'all, I gave that damn drum the business!

Kerry finished his audition and then we left, and as we rode back to Houston, I was thinking about PV, I even went to summer band practice at TSU that night, which was mainly for crabs, still thinking about PV. I was now stuck on PV. Saturday came, then Sunday came, I walked into my mother's room and said, "I'm going to PV" she said, "when?" I said, "tomorrow." All I heard was "ok". I called Kerry and told him to pick me up in the morning because it was Monday, the first day of band camp at Prairie View.

Those three days changed my life, because for three years I was destined for the Funk Train but now, I was about to crab the BOX. I walked into the band room and walked up on someone I knew, Freddy Player. Fred was the drum captain at Yates High, and I was the drum captain at Kashmere High. We battled all the time, but Fred and I were cool, the funny thing was, that when I walked up, I realized that they thought that Fred was me because they kept saying that he was down there Friday, and he kept saying no he wasn't, I said "nawl that was me." We all laughed. Then two cats from Dallas Skyline walked up and they were crabbing the BOX too, Larry and Homer, Tri-toms players. We were instant homies.

As the year progressed, it got harder and harder, we had earlier mornings and later nights. As we grew into a family, our family grew to include all of my BOX crab brothers and a crab sister. Vichelle was from Kansas City, she was hard, she took a lot and did a lot. She looked timid, but she didn't quit and she worked that snare. Shere was another Dallas cat, bass drummer, a real cool brother from Roosevelt High. This dude actually fell off the back of a car one night before a game, hit his head on the street, and we rushed him to the hospital. He got about fifteen stitches in his head and still marched in the game. He had a band hat on, while playing a BASS DRUM. I know that his head had to be hurting, but Shere was a soldier. Another cat that crabbed with us, was named Big Time. Big Time was on a whole other level than us "fresh out of high school crabs", you see, Big Time was about twenty-one years old, and had just transferred to PV from Bishop College in Dallas, Tx. He came in popular, he was Phi Beta Sigma and a Mason, so he hit the Yard running and he could play that bass drum, but he was still a CRAB in the BOX. Nobody ever told me that crabbing the BAND and crabbing the BOX were TWO totally different animals, GOOD LAWD, we didn't rest at all, but we were all in.

This was my new family, as well as all of my crab sisters and brothers throughout the entire band. From the first pep rally to the last game it was hard work but we survived it, but the crazy part about it was, we loved it. For all of the crab life that we were living in the band, we were living the college life and having big fun doing it. Every night that the band was practicing, there would be a few hundred students just hanging out at the band field just chilling, watching us practice, doing homework and mixing and mingling, it was a beautiful thing to see. Then all of those people would come to the game to see us at HALFTIME and we didn't let them down, we gave them our hearts every time, and they gave us their hearts too.

Those are great memories and if given the opportunity to change anything, I don't think that I could change much because being in the Band and being in the BOX as a freshman at PV, it gave us popularity and recognition and WE took full advantage of it. We were known on campus for dancing, getting the party hyped and having too much fun. Fred Player and Larry Johnson are my best friends, and if you saw one, you better believe that the other two were close by. We were the Three Amigo... "Uh oh there go those damn fools".. LOL. We were wild cats on the Yard, and even wilder on the drums.

When the PV McFunk BOX went to battle, we made sure that we won. Joe Jackson and Rodney Goods were our section leaders after David Rivers had to leave to go home for family reasons. Those dudes ran a tight ship. Andre Ceasar was the Sergeant at Arms, and he was cooler than a fan until we were at attention then this dude would turn into your worst nightmare, then turn back cool. LOL. Randy Razz inspired you to work harder, I can still hear him saying, "PERSERVERE!!! PERSERVERE!!!!" James Mays was the cool suave brother that was the cymbal captain, he never backed down, and then went on to become the High School Basketball Coach at South Oak Cliff High School and was most winningest coach in Dallas, Texas' history.

This was a peek into my first year at PV and I am pleased to brag that The BOX dominated the HBCU DrumWorld for the next three decades and inspired a lot of kids in a lot of cities in a lot of states do "IT" like the BOX. This was the beginning of "TECHNO-FUNK", TECHINCAL AND FUNK. When you get a chance, YouTube us, THE BOX 1976 thru 2010 and enjoy my joy.

About SKIP Wilson

I am a native Houstonian that fell in love with drums at an early age. It all started by me taking the pots and pans out of the cabinets and driving my mother crazy by constantly beating and beating while she was trying to cook. One day a friend of mine that lived five houses down from me, mother, threw away his Muppet's drum set. I saw it and I asked her if I could have it and she said yes. I was nine years old and this ironically was the start of a lifelong love of playing drums. Although that toy drum set didn't last but about two weeks, my love and passion flourished. The very next year, I was in the 6th grade and God gave me a band class and the band director, Mr. Hurdle let me choose the drums and I excelled. I later attended Kashmere Senior High School and the band director Mr. LeBlanc encouraged and demanded creativity so that's what we did, created. At Kashmere there were four brothers, the Taylor Boys Ricky, Pat, Mack, and Terry, that had all the style and pizazz that made for a pitri dish of creativity, style, love, and showmanship. We had a very good drumline. Then in 1987 I graduated and once again, God intervened, I enrolled at Prairie View A&M University and Majored in Psychology and Minored in English and this is where I met Professor George "Prof" Edwards and I "crabbed" (became a freshman member) In the greatest HBCU Band in the world. The drumline at Prairie View was called The PV McFunk BOX, "THE BOX" for short and they were the next level of playing and performing with a drum, I knew that I was home. I excelled, my drum skills and my creativity exploded and I helped create a style of drumming called "SHOWSTYLE". When my years of service to The BOX as far as performing was at its end, Prof. Edwards made me the the Assistant Percussion instructor assisting Professor Larry Jones with The BOX. This relationship lasted until May of 2009 when unfortunately Professor Edwards died from complications due to a car wreck. In 2003 I founded the Prairie View "Marching Storm" Band Alumni Association geared towards bridging the gap between the different eras of the band from the 1960's through the 2000's and raising much needed money that the band needed for equipment and scholarships. I've volunteered and taught at several at-risk High Schools in the Houston area and helped facilitate scholarships to multiple colleges and universities. Some of those schools are Madison High School 98-99, Thurgood Marshall High School 2002-2006, North Forest High School 2009-to present, Alto Senior High School 2015 to present and I also consult and teach at Forest Brook Middle School which is the feeder school to North Forest High School. This was journey and I will do it as long as God wants me to.

Dr. Kathryn D. Kelly, MD.

The Medicine of HBCU Band Participation
Dr. Kathryn D. Kelly, MD
Physician Owner, Kelly Collaborative Medicine
Howard University

When I walked onto campus for freshmen orientation, I had no idea what I would do next in band. All I knew was that I wanted to be a part of it. When the band started to play with a mix of old-heads and freshmen, I was drawn to it. I went that afternoon and asked how to join. I was blessed to be at Howard University on a full scholarship and a part of the six-year accelerated BS-MD program. I was taking twenty-one credit hours and I knew going home wasn't an option. But neither was sitting out from the marching band. Fast forward a few months, I was a member of the clarinet section and had sat next to my future husband on a flight cross country. April 22, 1998 marked a pivotal point in my band career and in my life. I was initiated into the Eta Delta Chapter of Tau Beta Sigma, National Honorary Band Sorority, Incorporated!

I remember distinctly the moment I learned that going to an HBCU was an option. The twin musician in my high school band talked all the time about going to FAMU to play in the band. They, in fact, entered in the fall of 1996 as a trumpet and saxophone player. Another close friend talked at length about his family history of attendance at Fisk University. His passion for what an HBCU could offer influenced my decision to apply to Howard. I grew up watching FAMU and Bethune-Cookman participate in the Florida Classic every year in Tampa. My band experience had been core style. I was mesmerized by the energy of FAMU and the precision of Bethune-Cookman College. FAMU was fun, but BCC was perfection of tone and visual execution of the formations. This was my only exposure to HBCUs and their music programs at that time.

My journey consists of many twists and turns. I was a teenage mother at the age of fifteen. However, I managed to do very well in high school. My mother allowed me to continue to participate in the band. I marched the entire season during my pregnancy during my sophomore year in my school's superior-rated marching band. I went on to be a drum major, but I had a very rough senior year. That year was filled with mistakes that could have derailed my future. My counselors always pushed me to apply to NYU, Boston College, Emory, University of Florida and Baylor. Those schools were considered the best in pursuing my dream of becoming a physician. Band was actually not a part of the equation. I got into those programs, but only applied to one HBCU: Howard University. I interviewed for their BS-MD program.

I received a full scholarship to Howard University, with acceptance into the BS-MD program. However, I was devastated that I did not get into my first choice: Washington University in St. Louis. I didn't get accepted because of those senior year obstacles. Although I got hundreds of thousands of dollars in scholarship money, Howard had the most to offer in terms of my long-term goals. I arrived at Howard University, thinking it would be like high school. I would be popular among the students, specifically in leadership. I would be one of the top students in my class. I also knew I would be in the band. My mother allowed me to leave my then two-and-a-half-year-old daughter with her and travel almost 1,000 miles from home to Washington, D.C. to be a young adult and focus on my education. I know now that this was the greatest gift I could have ever received. This gift allowed me to catapult myself to the next level of success.

Howard University was a rude awakening for my ego. I was not the smartest. I was not the most popular. I had not been invited to participate in band camp because I had not expressed interest previously. Also, I wasn't a stand-out musician in high school. I had to redefine myself. I could no longer be the "smart black kid" because *everyone* was black. I had to redefine "Black" as a noun, not an adjective. I had to see who I was as Kathryn, not as a teen mom or a "token". Band helped me find my home at Howard.

Now, like any family, you figure out how you fit in. I felt that being a woman in an HBCU band meant different things than in high school. In high school, I could distinguish myself as a leader through the role of drum major. In college, I felt quickly like that role was out of reach. I was not "tall and slim," and I could not do a backbend. Although there had been female drum majors before my time, I did not feel the exposure to their influence as I do now. It should be noted that there were extraordinary women in *every* section. What I did see was women in the band leading, and leading well, through participation in Tau Beta Sigma. I knew when I watched them, that this was what I wanted to do. It was how I could lead.

I marched in the Howard University "Showtime" Marching Band for four years and participated in pep band and concert band during that time. I played clarinet (my principal instrument), baritone horn and bassoon. I took on major leadership roles in Tau Beta Sigma both on the chapter and district level, including being the district president my senior year. Yet, I was spreading myself too thin. I was dean of the spring 2001 line, president of Beta Kappa Chi Scientific Honor Society, district president, trying to finish two majors in Biology and Anthropology, and working two jobs. I remember oversleeping for a pep band performance and missing my biggest Beta Kappa Chi responsibility because I was exhausted. This is when I realized I had to set priorities. I could not be everything to everyone. Leadership is not about leading everything. It's about leading *well* in something. Marching band at an HBCU will highlight your flaws. It will show when you have not practiced enough or when you are not focused. I had those days as a senior.

After graduation, I continued my participation in Tau Beta Sigma, holding numerous positions. I was honored to be elected as the 36th National President of the organization in 2015, and I am the only National President from a HBCU, and only the second African

American President in the sorority's almost 75-year-history. The HBCU experience shaped my approach at the national level in many ways. As a part of a single-sex chapter, I never felt like I needed to be a part of a co-educational fraternity. However, I had to be able to look at the perspective of others and not let my biases affect my decisions as a president on why females chose to be in other organizations or males choose to be in a sorority. I was confident in myself as a person because I did the work to define Kathryn outside of my blackness. This allowed me to let others do the same when I came to their gender definition, race, ethnicity or sexual orientation (which is actually none of my business). Although I did feel some restriction as a woman in an HBCU band, overall, I felt like attending an HBCU and participating in the band helped me eliminate gender roles and demand equality in what I could contribute to any situation.

Participating in an HBCU marching band was one of the hardest jobs of my life. We practiced every day. We performed every weekend and we had to push ourselves for perfection as a team. As a physician, residency felt easier because I already had the work ethic as a scholar, musician, and Tau Beta Sigma member. I can organize a fundraiser, run a meeting, organize a major event, and manage an investment portfolio because of my participation in marching band and my leadership in Tau Beta Sigma. I am comfortable being authentically Kathryn because, in those settings, Kathryn was indeed good enough. I was never excused from my failures. I was held accountable, and I worked to improve on my performance doing 8 to 5 on the field, and living the principles prescribed in the five qualities and eight essential factors of Tau Beta Sigma.

Although many on the outside may have questioned us as an HBCU, specifically in Tau Beta Sigma, we know the strength we possess. We know that our cultural connection to the HBCU experience adds diversity and insight to any organization. The "flavor" we bring builds bridges of friendship and sisterhood. The connection to the struggle gives us compassion. The dedication to equality gives us passion for a lifelong commitment to the things that are important in our lives.

Without band, we are a shell of our potential.

Without music, we are only a partially full vessel.

About Dr. Kathryn D. Kelly, MD.

Dr. Kathryn Garrett Kelly is Board Certified Internal Medicine Physician practicing in Silver Spring Maryland. Dr. Kelly was a member of the Howard University "Showtime" Marching Band and Pep Bands from the Fall of 1997 to the Spring of 2001 where she played Clarinet and Baritone Horn and member of the University concert band where she played Bassoon. Dr. Kelly received her Bachelors of Science Degree in Biology and Bachelors of Arts Degree in Anthropology from Howard University in 2001. After graduation, Dr. Kelly worked toward a Masters in Education Degree while teaching High School Science in the Bronx, NY. Dr. Kelly received her Doctor of Medicine Degree from the Howard University College of Medicine in 2007 and completed her Internal Medicine Residency at Washington Hospital Center from 2007-2010, staying on for an additional year as a Chief Medicine Resident from 2010-2011. Dr. Kelly is currently the owner and president of Kelly Collaborative Medicine with a focus on Primary Care.

Dr. Kelly was initiated into the Eta Delta Chapter of Tau Beta Sigma, National Honorary Band Sorority, Inc. in April of 1998 serving as Chapter President, Parliamentarian, and Vice President for Membership. On the district level, Dr. Kelly served as District Treasurer (1999-2000), District President (2000-2001), NEDAA Vice President for TBS (2001-2006), and District Counselor (2006-2009). Dr. Kelly served on the National Level as National Vice President for Special Projects (2009-2011), National Vice President for Colonization and Membership (2013-2015), and the 36th National President from 2015-2017. Dr. Kelly also served on the Board of Trustees as the Immediate Past National President from 2017-2019.

Dr. Kelly currently serves as the Treasurer and Board Member for Girls Health Ed, and organization whose mission is to educated girls so they can make empowered decisions about their health. Additionally, Dr. Kelly serves as the Vice President of the Howard University Medical Alumni Association Board of Trustees.

Dr. Kelly, is married to Jackie Kelly, Jr., also a Howard University graduate and "Showtime" Alumnus of the Percussion Section.   The Kellys have 3 children: Ajzha (26), Jackson (13), and Reagan (6).

Deena Smith

From the Band Room to the Boardroom

Deena Smith

North Carolina Central University

Being a member of an HBCU marching band molded me into the woman I am today. It's a bold statement, I know! I'd like to offer my experience as a roadmap or cautionary tale… take from it what you need.

When I think of my four years as a member of the NCCU Sound Machine Marching Band, I can't help but think about the S.O.S. Band songs, "S.O.S." and "Take Your Time (Do It Right)." These songs are powerful music. They jam. They make you want to move your body. When it hits just right, you feel it in your soul. I think the messages in these songs illuminate two principles that have guided me through college and beyond: the need to take your time to ensure excellence and being able to recognize success so you can create a path toward your own fulfillment. I am grateful for marching band being my village during my collegiate years – providing signposts by which to measure my growth, giving me room to push boundaries, offering me a safe space to land when I made mistakes, allowing me to soar, and covering me when I needed to heal. The lessons below carried me from the band room to the boardroom.

Growing up in Prince George's County, Maryland, I was surrounded by Black excellence before it became part of our common vernacular. My community was full of beautiful, educated, impressive Black people. My upbringing led me to believe we were all part of W.E.B. DuBois' "Talented Tenth." I was surrounded by Black executives, entrepreneurs, educators, healers, artists and administrators. Every Sunday, my pastor somehow found a way to work in his HBCU alma mater into the sermon. We learned Black history in school and made sure public institutions honored the contributions Black Americans made to society. It wasn't uncommon to learn that we lived next door to a trailblazer.

I attended a science and technology high school with rigorous academic standards and explicit expectations for students to attend good colleges. After ninth grade, band and orchestra took a backseat to other activities. I joined JROTC, danced on the pom-pom squad, and I was involved in just about every youth ministry at church. I was invited to attend dance and cheer camps with professional squads, and I spent my summers nerding out at engineering camps on college campuses. While our school had no formal community service requirement, the value of interacting with our neighbors and cultivating academic excellence was ingrained.

A classmate and I petitioned school leaders to allow us to create an enrichment program for girls in grades 4 through 6 at our neighboring elementary school. Not only did we tutor the students, but we grew the program to include a drill team where the girls performed at schools, churches and in parades. In ROTC, I was selected to serve as Honor Guard commander. Our color guard and drill teams racked up national title after national title. I was booked and busy! I had this high school thing on lock! How hard could college be?

I took a lot of time weighing my options and I became overwhelmed when it came to choosing a college. I applied to big schools, small schools, west coast schools and schools "down south." Coming from a family of Aggies, Belles, Bears, Broncos, Eagles, Wildcats, and all manner of menagerie, I understood it was a privilege to attend an HBCU, not a last resort. As graduation drew near, I was no closer to deciding. I seriously considered enlisting in the Air Force. My dad was an Army veteran and my grandfather served in the Navy, part of the historic B-1 Band. Fate intervened and, after a phone call from Mr. Xavier Cason, Director of Bands at North Carolina Central University, I accepted the invitation to take my talents to Durham. It never entered my mind to be in a college marching band, HBCU or otherwise.

I got a reality check very quickly in the form of band camp. But first, let's talk about the campus of NCCU. There are hills and a lot of stairs. At this time, the campus was in the middle of a construction boom, so there were detours everywhere. I was greatly surprised when I got settled in my dorm and had to navigate my way around campus, which seemed really easy in a car. In actuality, it was a strenuous workout by foot. There were no shuttles to ferry us from dorm room to cafeteria to downtown. We hoofed it. Making it from our dorm to the practice field for early morning practice was a task. That's actually how I met my best friends. We were all about to be late for the very first morning of practice at band camp!

We rushed out of the rooms, pressed to get ahead of each other, and ended up in a tangled heap falling down the stairs! My besties remember this story way better than I do because I wasn't worried about making friends or being nice. I just wanted to get where I was going. However, I sure learned a lesson that day. I didn't get to practice any earlier than the young ladies I tried to push out of my way. *We all fell down. And we all got up.* We ended up marching in the same section, and we have been indelible parts of each other's lives since that day. These are my sisters for life, and I thank God we ran into each other that day.

My experience as a member of the NCCU Sound Machine Marching Band challenged me to grow from an inquisitive teenager to a problem-solving young adult. It was invigorating to attend a liberal arts college that encouraged intellectual curiosity. College was like a choose-your-own-adventure book. Being in the band forced me to live by a schedule. I had to eat, practice, study, attend class, practice, perform, and make time for a social life. I took my time deciding on a major, soaking up the academic experience. I had the freedom to take classes at nearby universities and take full advantage of the numerous nearby libraries. I studied abroad, participated in academic groups, and presided over the Metro Club – an organization for students from the metropolitan Washington, D.C. area.

I also got involved in student government to make sure band concerns were represented when student affairs funding and activity scheduling decisions took place. We had band members in the various fraternities and sororities on campus, and we worked hard to ensure good relationships were maintained across the yard. So, when the band needed something, we had a strong base of support. I was in a constant cycle of building up and activating goodwill from relationships with organizations, administrators and faculty members to make inroads with decision-makers. I've found this practice of identifying stakeholders, establishing relationships, advocating for your cause, and helping others is key to creating meaningful connections. I use these skills daily in my professional life.

After marching two years in the clarinet section, I was ready for a new challenge. We needed to replenish our mellophone section. So, along with one of my Tau Beta Sigma line sisters, we answered the call. We stepped up to catch hell! No one else volunteered, but everyone had something to say. My retort was always, "You are welcome to join the section since you have so much to say about it." I found it funny that none of the existing brass players, many of whom had been playing brass since fifth grade, offered to switch. I was furious! However, I let that passion push me. This was truly my first experience in facing adversity – acquiring a new skill, overcoming uncertainty, addressing personal dynamics, and succeeding or failing in a very public way. Was I a great mello player? Not the point. I gave it my all. I did my job and allowed the leadership to determine whether or not I needed to be there. I played mello my final two years in the band.

I joined Tau Beta Sigma National Honorary Band Sorority in 1997 and became a Life Member in 2001. The sorority introduced me to student leaders from across our district, as well as across the nation. I attended my first Kappa Kappa Psi & Tau Beta Sigma National Convention in 1999, meeting brothers and sisters from all types of band programs. This amazing experience taught me that our programs shared similar struggles, joys, traditions and aspirations. It helped me dig deeper to become a better bandsman and a more dedicated leader. It's been an honor to be selected to serve Tau Beta Sigma through my chapter, in the alumni association, and as an elected national officer.

In band, as in life, you are participating in a shared experience. You tune your instrument to blend in with the ensemble. You adjust your arms so there is no distinction between you and the person behind you. You will learn to negotiate. You will learn to find the answer that fits the problem. You will learn to aim for perfection and make real-time adjustments to achieve that goal. You can apply the lessons learned on the field to all facets of life. When you write that paper, when you submit that proposal, when you make a speech or pitch an idea – know your audience. Take the time to invest in relationships – and remember that they are reciprocal. Give of yourself, your talent and your skills. Create opportunities for other people to shine, so you both grow. And always, always, always acknowledge your supporters. It costs you nothing to say, "Thank you!"

You may have heard the expression, "If you want to make God laugh, tell Him your plans!" Well, I am a couple of decades into performing a side-splitting comedic masterpiece. I had no plan to be in an HBCU marching band; yet, I count involvement in the Sound Machine as a defining chapter in my life. Landing at NCCU created space for me to indulge in academic curiosities, learn how to network with and advocate for others, and push past barriers. Time management, accountability, reliability, and the importance of networking and nurturing relationships are valuable skills that I employ every day. I know to treat people well. That person you step over, trying to get to your goal, just might be the one to help you reach your goal. Keep pushing and find your supporters. Keep your eyes on the prize. Maintain a strategy to get there, and don't get discouraged. Honed from four years of marching in NCCU's Sound Machine, I know that I know to accomplish any goal, I need to take my time and do it right. I've learned to listen for the sounds of success, to see it up close and personal—so I know how to achieve it on my own journey to truth and service.

About Deena Smith

Deena TaKara Smith is driven by her love of people and the desire to transform knowledge into actionable power. It is no surprise that she landed in the field of librarianship after graduating with a Bachelor of Arts (History) from North Carolina Central University. Upon obtaining a Master of Library/Information Science from the University of Maryland, she gained experience in a variety of libraries where she identified, selected and implemented technologies which connected users with information.

Ms. Smith currently manages a federal law library where the primary audience is federal judges and court staff. Passionate about the field of librarianship and its applications across other industries, she has presented at the American Library Association, American Association of Law Libraries, Federal Court Librarians Conference, Federal Library and Information Network, Joint Conference of Librarians of Color, and other conferences.

Deena provides direct service to empower underserved members of her community, focusing her service on families and literacy. The inaugural recipient of Thursday Network's Spirit of Service Luminary Award, Deena has also been recognized as one of NCCU's "40 Under 40" and Prince George's County "Forty Under 40." Deena is a Life Member of Tau Beta Sigma National Honorary Band Sorority and serves on the Board of Directors for the Junior League of Washington. She is a third-generation legacy of Zeta Phi Beta Sorority, Inc.

Gerard L. Howard

Creations of a Bandhead
Gerard L. Howard
Jackson State University

During my freshman year at Jackson State University, I was part of some of the greatest battles our band had seen that decade. Our matchup versus Florida A&M in 1995 rekindled the rivalry between both bands. Our battle against Southern University's Human Jukebox was one of the longest, most intense battles in the HBCU band world. It ended with both bands exiting a locked and pitch-black stadium at 1 a.m., as well as a clash against a 250+ piece Alcorn Braves Band in its prime. I'd come to Jackson State on a partial band scholarship, but I was able to transition to a research fellowship by the end of my freshman year.

When speaking the program's coordinator about playing in the band, he mentioned that they preferred I just focus on school. So, I went with it. The fellowship covered tuition, out-of-state fees, room and board, books and my meal plan. I even had a $600 stipend per month. It was a full ride. Consequently, I wrote a letter to each of the band directors, thanking them for recruiting me and giving me an opportunity to play. I explained to them my new venture and asked if I could work with the band in a different capacity. I had taught myself to build websites that year and proposed building the band's first website.

It was the mid-90s and the World Wide Web, as we know it now, was in its infancy. As it turns out, in addition to being head band director, Dr. Liddell was a programmer and took me up on the offer.

During the fall of 1996, I bought a point-and-shoot camera and began traveling with the band to take pictures for its first website. I had no experience in photography; however, I wanted my finished work to look like something that should be published in *Sports Illustrated*.

On the field, there were professional photographers from The Associated Press, BET, local newspapers, television stations, as well as various sporting news outlets—all covering the HBCU football experience. Yet, no one covered the game exclusively from the band's perspective. They would shoot halftime and the dancers, not the other battle that was occurring in the stands between the bands.

By the end of the semester, I had taken pictures from the entire season from games and Battles of the Bands. I didn't do it just for Jackson State, but the bands they were performing against, as well. I was ready to create the Sonic Boom's first website. The band's site went live in the spring of '97. Among its highlights were a photo gallery of all the bands I had captured on film the previous semester, along with a guestbook. After seeing the site for the first time, Dr. Liddell loved it. However, he promptly told me to take down the pictures of the other bands. I tried to make a case for it, but he told me this was our site, not the site for other bands. On a personal note, I'd advocated for showing the other bands because, as far as I knew, there was no other place on the internet to see pictures of various HBCU bands.

The site also featured a guestbook, which was the in thing at the time. The concept behind a guestbook was that visitors would come to your site and leave their names and a message. Typically, alumni and fans left messages for the band, but that would soon change. Shortly after the guestbook went live, bandsmen from other schools started using it as a tool to communicate with each other. Alabama A&M would leave comments for Alabama State. Southern would leave comments for Grambling—all on JSU's guestbook. There was obviously a need for bandsmen to have a place to communicate with each other. It was also a place on the internet where people could view professional quality photos of HBCU marching bands.

Thus, I began creating the internet's first dot.com for Black college marching bands. My aim was to create an ESPN-like site for bands where people could go to watch highlights of the bands soon after the game. Without the right equipment, posting video on the web at that time was a tedious task. Most people still had dial-up connections, making downloading videos difficult. So, I chose to use photography and audio, which was easier to get on the web at the time.

Launched as blackcollegebands.com in the fall of 1998, the site quickly became a place where the band community could talk noise before and after the game, as well as see photos and hear audio of the battles. The site's name was changed to marchingsport.com in the early 2000s and continued to thrive.

Following the games, I created pages with photo and audio highlights. One such time, I was labeling highlights from the Jackson State vs. Southern game. I decided to label it as something other than "Southern vs. Jackson State 2000X." From the band community's standpoint, the game was a classic. I looked at the nicknames for each band: The Sonic Boom of the South and the Human Jukebox. I thought, "Juke Boom, Boombox" and labeled the footage from the game, "The Boombox Classic."

I didn't realize that it had caught on until the following year. I was talking with a bandhead from Atlanta who, in conversation, randomly said, "The Boombox Classic was going to be tight this year." I said, "Wow!" to myself and knew that the phrase had caught on. It's been called that by the band community ever since.

In 2005, I began including video highlights, in addition to my photography and audio coverage. Bandheads went crazy with being able to not just talk about what happened at the game, but also having the ability to watch the battle as evidence immediately after the game. It became immensely popular. The next year, I made plans to improve my presentation. YouTube was in its infancy at this time, and video sharing sites were becoming more popular.

In May of 2006, I launched The Marching Network, a video-on-demand website for HBCU marching bands. By that time, more people were getting broadband connections, so putting video on the web was easier. That fall, The Marching Network became the hub of

HBCU band videos on the internet. Bandheads would go to games, come back and place their videos on the network.

The Zero Quarter was also another popular term I came up with during the Marching Network days. I was trying to label the battles that took place before The Star-Spangled Banner. The Fifth Quarter was the term used to describe the post-game battles between bands. It was also the name of another popular band site. At the time, I labeled the before-game footage as "Pre-Game" and my Fifth Quarter footage as "Post-Game" to avoid using the name the Fifth Quarter. Since Christy and Mike (the owners of the5thquarter.com) already had the 5th, I figured I'd label my pre-game footage as "The Zero" for zero quarter. Other videographers started using the term to label their pre-game footage, and it was soon adopted by the band community as a whole.

The Marching Network thrived for several years, declining as YouTube became more popular. Added to that, the video hosting provider I was using merged with another company and discontinued its services. By then, social networks were a new thing. It was time for a new adventure: bandhead.org. Bandhead merged much of what had been popular at the time into one package, a discussion community and video site in one. At its peak, the site had over 20,000 members and over 40,000 videos of HBCU and high school marching bands.

In the 2010s, the internet shifted heavily toward social networks. With Facebook leading the way, many users began leaving traditional web communities for those on major social networking platforms. YouTube had also come into its own by then. The band community transitioned there for HBCU band videos. I followed the YouTube trend and started a channel that has since garnered over 100,000 subscribers. It has become an international hub for those seeking to view the HBCU band experience.

With over two decades of covering the HBCU band experience, my work has been seen by tens of millions of viewers. It is almost impossible for someone to look into HBCU bands and not have seen my work. It has helped to recruit generations of bandsmen. They started off as high school students and went on to become college band members, high school directors and even HBCU band directors.

Over the years, I've had work featured in print, online and in televised projects including: The New York Times, Vibe Magazine, Stanley Nelson's HBCU Documentary, Tell Them We are Rising, as well as the Music Crossroads video exhibition at The Smithsonian's National Museum of African American History and Culture.

The journey continues.

About Gerard L. Howard

Gerard Howard has spent nearly two decades documenting the world of black college bands. After starting the internet's dotcom for Black college bands (blackcollegebands.com) in 1998, Howard spends weekends every fall traveling from city to city showcasing the legacy of HBCU Bands. "Before I began covering bands, most media outlets on the field were only covering sports. My focus was strictly the bands," says Howard. "As a kid I used to watch HBCU football on BET every Saturday night just to see the bands. Where BET ended is where I began. Growing up in New Orleans, besides Southern and Grambling, we didn't know what other bands sounded like. We would only hear rumors of them. My job was to show others what they looked and sounded like."

Since that time, Howard has photographed hundreds of games and has expanded to documenting via film. Added to that, he has interviewed legendary band greats such as William P. Foster of Florida A&M University, Isaac Greggs of Southern University, as well as Jackson State University's Lewis Liddell.

Self-trained, Howard is known for an in-the-trenches style of photography. A gritty approach that shows the intensity and aggression of sport that he calls The Marchingsport. As a result, he has had work featured in Vibe magazine and is also frequently used as a reference by national publications when they cover bands. Furthermore, Gerard's work has been featured in Stanley Nelson's documentary, *Tell Them We are Rising,* as well as in the permanent collection of the Mississippi Museum of Art. In 2018, one of his videos was included in an HBCU exhibit at the Smithsonian's Museum of African American History. Because of his attention to detail and high-quality videography, his videos are often noticed and shared by celebrities via social media and major online publications.

With a new-found interest in art, Howard's subjects expanded to fine art photography and resulted in his participation in solo and group shows in Jackson and New Orleans. As a nature and landscape photographer, Gerard has traveled the world from Iceland to Antarctica building a portfolio of both well-known landmarks and cityscapes.

Howard's current sites include bandhead.org, a social networking site for bands, and MARCHINGSPORT.COM., which features his most up-to-date and archived videos of HBCU Bands.

A member of the Alpha Phi Alpha Fraternity, Inc., Howard currently lives in Jackson, Mississippi, where he works as a webmaster. He can also be heard Monday-Friday on WJSU as an on-air jazz radio personality. In 2014, his show Jazz Reflections was also put into syndication on SiriusXM (Channel 142). He also performs as a bass drummer with Southern Komfort Brass Band.

Joseph Beard

A Fixed Fight
Joseph Beard

Jackson State University
Johnson C. Smith University

It was Friday October 17, 1997 in Jackson, Mississippi. Our time to prepare for one of our toughest rivals in the Human Jukebox of Southern University was coming to an end as Saturday marched closer. We spent many long nights on the old football field, making sure the halftime show was full of enthusiasm and making sure each formation was precise. Every time there was the slightest mistake, Assistant Band Director Edward Duplessis yelled at us, "Even Ray Charles can see that is not right! Take it to the endzone!" This meant take it from the top. We spent even longer nights in the band hall, making sure the book was tight and that every song was memorized like the backs of our hands. We also had to make sure we were conditioned to play until the sun came up the following day after the game. Assistant Band Director Michael Magruder exclaimed, "You got to handle your business 'cause Southern is coming for your heads tomorrow!"

The rivalry between Jackson State and Southern is one of the best in the world. When the two bands get together, wanting to show up and show out is automatic. To close practice for the week, Head Band Director Lewis Liddell, who marched with my father, Joe L. Beard, at Jackson State in the 1960s, when the Jackson State University Marching Band was called 'The Best Band in the Land' and directed by the legend William W. Davis, told us, "We are in a perpetual state of readiness!" This meant we had to get mentally prepared for the battle right now, not wait until the next day to start preparing for battle. After all the preparation, we still came together and completed sectionals, which was a time to further fine tune the music for the show, each song of the book, and whatever sectional fanfare would be deployed in the stands during the game. This was important, not only for the next day, but for the young people. Whether they would be watching live or watching on VHS band tapes, they had to decide where they wanted to march when they were of age. It would be a long night, but the legacy that we would tell our grandchildren was at stake. We had to rise to the challenge for the sake of our program and for the bragging rights to another premiere program.

On the morning of October 18, 1997, it was time to report to the band room with our uniforms in hand and our minds still in a perpetual state of readiness. Assistant Band Director Paul Adams told us, "You got to have some fun today. This rivalry is something that you will remember for the rest of your lives. So, loosen up, smile, and have a good time." Director of Percussion, William Bethea, walked through the War and Thunder ranks, saying, "Get ready for a long night! This is what you came to Jackson State for!" Standard tradition before leaving the campus was the drum majors coming to the front of the band to call roll for the thirty-two squads to make sure each member was present for the field show. Then, we recited the band pledge and the singing of Jackson Fair. It was time to go to war. After the bus ride to Memorial Stadium, we got off the bus and lined up to march into the stadium. The Boom always got there a little late to make sure there were enough fans present to see the blue and white pom-poms flashing as we marched into the stadium. This is known as one of the best moments in marching band allure. To see the Sonic Boom marching while playing *Get Ready* by the Temptations gave our fans and our football team the extra momentum they needed for the day. It was a special moment for the visiting fans to immediately understand that they were in for a tough fight. The Boom usually got to the game before the other band, but this day was different. The Human Jukebox was already in their seats. We had no idea what we were in store for as the rivalry unfolded that day.

The tradition continued as the drum majors blew their whistles to tap off *Get Ready*. The 'tuba dawgs' played the introduction that made all the Jackson State fans stand to their feet. The blue and white pom-poms started to electrify the air. I had been in a couple of games up to this point in the year, but that day made my skin vibrate like all the years growing up watching the Boom play. The dream my father had for me, and him taking me to Memphis, Chicago and Indianapolis all made sense. The purpose had culminated in just a few tweets of the whistle.

Playing note for note, I was in my lifelong dream. We performed *Get Ready* as we marched into the stadium, getting closer and closer to our fierce enemy, who was already in the stands. I happened to look up at Southern, and the brass section started to stand up. I thought to myself, *Why are they doing that?* We were nearing the end of *Get Ready*, the part right before the piccolo solo that precedes the entire band screaming, "Sonic Boom!" Then, our beloved drum cadence 'Series' kicked in, which supercharged the band with plums swinging in unison and the Boom marching 90s ready to hit the ramp. The piccolo solo began. The next thing we know, we heard the smashing brick of Juke brass, "Hay in the middle of the barn...smoking on...hay in the middle of the barn!" *What in the hell was that?*

The Southern fans came alive and got excited, as if we were in Baton Rouge. It surprised everyone in the stadium. It created a story that would be told for years from many different vantage points. I looked to my right and in front of me at the rest of the trumpet section. Southern was at full mass, playing on us. *So, that is why they got here early!* None of us were expecting it. Most of the band either stopped marching or got off step and lost the rhythm. We were in the middle of an attack! Southern was playing on us in full disrespect, in our home stadium, trying to make us look like fools. Not to mention the fact that they waited until the piccolo solo, the softest part of the song to do it. This was calculated and planned, and they wanted to make an example of us.

Instantly, the Boom bonded. That bond would be cemented for years to come. All the upperclassmen started to keep the beat by chanting "Left! Left! Left! Left!" I am sure Southern thought we would totally break down and just start walking to the stands with our tails between our legs. With the repetition of playing *Get Ready* already being in our blood, the next thing I heard was the four taps of War and Thunder starting one of the greatest cadences of all time. We were led into the stands, despite being under constant attack from the Jukebox. What Southern did not plan for was that we would get angry, and that is exactly what happened. Our beloved drum section started to blast 'Series' louder than ever before. It got the Boom hype. The surprise of the first note was all they got in pulling this stunt. Due to the angle of where they were in the stands, their bells were pointing to the other side of the field. So, while they were playing, we were under them. Most of the sound traveled over our heads and it allowed us to recover quickly.

Since *Hay* was more of a tuba-break song, it was not a full song that they could continue to play to make us lose step. It was the chorus of the song and nothing but their tubas playing, which WT compensated. They continued to play the hook of the song. But once we hit the ramp, they woke up a giant. I must admit that it made the battle more intense. Though very disrespectful, it was a moment to be remembered for the ages. It was like in an action movie when the hero is at the brink of defeat, only to be inspired and conquer the adversary to win in the end. What really showed their fear was how they started to put their hats on at the end of the fourth quarter. They did not stay to battle for the fifth quarter, like a kid sucker punching a bigger kid and running behind a teacher to not face the wrath of their action. If you do something like play on us marching in, you must stay and finish the fight. But the Jukes ran as soon as the clock went out. To this day, people see the video and talk about how, in those few seconds, the Boom got off step and how surprised we were. The Jukebox got what they wanted in a cheap shot. But, at the end of the game, it felt good to play our book on them while they walked out of the stadium. It is not how you start the race, but how you finish it.

Sonic Boom forever!

About Joseph Beard

Joseph Beard was born and raised in St. Louis, Mo. He attended Johnson C. Smith University and marched for the International Institution of Sound in 1996. Joseph then transferred the following year to Jackson State University and marched for the Sonic Boom of the South from 1997-1999, where he graduated in 2001 with a Bachelor of Arts in History, and then went to graduate school at Indiana University of Pennsylvania graduating in 2003 with a Master of Science in Geography. His parents also both attended HBCUs - Joe Leonard Beard (Jackson State class of 1966) and Natalie Von Kennedy Beard (Spelman College class of 1971).

In 2011, Joseph started the Marching Podcast (http://themarchingpodcast.com/), which is a network consisting of four podcast series that help spread knowledge about marching bands at Historically Black Colleges (The 90 Degree Show), high school students that are planning to march for HBCUs (National Signing Day for Marching Bands), band directors that have written books (The Directors Series), and people who have graduated from HBCUs that are doing positive things in the world including people that have made a positive influence on his life (Choppin' It Up). During the podcast episodes the network runs commercials to help to spread information about businesses that the network believes in and wants to support. Joseph is currently working as a software engineer for Environmental Science and Research Institute in Redlands, CA, a teacher's assistant for 'Elements of Cartographic Design' at University of California Riverside Extension in Riverside, CA, and an adjunct professor for 'Physical Geography' and 'Introduction to Geography Information Systems' for Crafton Hills College in Yucaipa, CA.

Dr. Jorim & Aja Reid

The Reids Marching at "100" Percent Excellence: A FAMU Rattler Story

Dr. Jorim & Aja Reid

Florida A&M University

After making the final decision to attend FAMU because of the esteemed School of Business & Industry, there was no way I would matriculate through the "Highest of 7 Hills" without being in "that number." Before my arrival, I had only seen the Marching 100 perform once, but that was enough to close the deal! It was the fall of 1994 at the inaugural Atlanta High School Battle of the Bands. I grew up in Atlanta. So, the largest college band I'd witnessed in person was the Marching Wolverines of Morris Brown College. From the moment FAMU entered the stadium and walked through Morris Brown's ranks (which was an HBCU band no-no), I was mesmerized. When I heard 20th Century Fanfare, my mouth gasped. My eyes widened. The sound was powerful, yet beautiful. From the drill to Aaron Hall's "I Miss You" and seeing them execute a dance routine with full sound, I became an instant fan. Little did I know that my future husband (Jorim) also performed that day as drum major.

Fast forward to August 1998. It was the first day of pre-drill (what other HBCU bands call Band Camp), and I was super nervous! I never attended any of the FAMU high school summer band camps and knew *no one*. I had only received my music packet a week before arriving, so I had a *lot* to learn. At the freshmen meeting, Dr. White (Director of Bands) asked all former drum majors and section leaders to stand. I just knew that I would be one of few drum majors. So, you can imagine my surprise when 90% of the room stood up. From that moment, it began to register what I aspired to join. Everything was done in excellence. How we entered the band room, the expectation of perfection in every practice, greatness was the standard. We were required to learn our freshmen brothers' and sisters' information, including their full name and hometown.

We had to know all the band staff's and drum majors' information, the FAMU Alma Mater, Florida Song and the band motto. The band motto still sticks with me. It truly speaks to the "Transfer of Learning" Dr. William P. Foster (Founder of the FAMU Marching 100) instilled:

Qualities to live by to guide our thoughts and to rule our actions/lives:

- "Highest Quality of CHARACTER"
- "Achievement in ACADEMICS"
- "Attainment in LEADERSHIP"
- "Perfection in MUSICIANSHIP"
- "Precision in MARCHING"
- "Dedication to SERVICE"

The Florida A&M University Bands, a role model of excellence.

This became my why. That season, I built lifelong relationships with friends who are now family. I met my husband, and I learned that *nothing* was too hard if I committed to seeing it through. Was it difficult? Yes! Were all the long hours of practice in the hot Florida sun worth it? Absolutely! It built character. It taught me the importance of commitment and working in teams. It shaped me into the woman I am today. I had opportunities to serve in leadership roles (Freshman Class Parliamentarian, Song Leader, Business Manager, and Marching 100 HS Band Camp, Head Dorm Counselor) and work on teams (Show Planning Committee and Dance Routine Committee). I pledged Tau Beta Sigma National Honorary Band Sorority and held additional leadership roles (Song Leader, Vice President, Southeast District Convention Coordinator).

Even though we have both graduated, the grit, perseverance and standard of excellence remains. Jorim and I navigate our professional careers and raise our children by being a "Role Model of Excellence" in all we do. In all duties, whether it be cleaning their rooms, playing a sport, or completing a school project, excellence is the expectation. Ninety-nine and a half won't do in the Reid household. We expect the best! Quite frankly, this attitude of excellence permeated throughout all organizations at FAMU. There was a process for *everything* (gospel choir, dance troupe, sorority/fraternity), which I felt built character. The process of becoming a member of the "Incomparable" FAMU Marching 100 was one of the hardest, yet the most rewarding experiences I have ever completed. I wouldn't change a thing.

I was still undecided about what college I would attend in my high school senior year. I was offered a band scholarship to FAMU my junior year after performing at the Florida Band Masters Association State Festival on the University of Miami campus. Dr. Julian E. White, the Associate Director of Bands at that time, offered me an oboe scholarship on the spot, possibly thinking that I was a senior because I was wearing my drum major uniform. I was star-struck because the FAMU band director I watched on so many BET band videos, who wore the iconic "F" band director's hat, found me to talk. I grew up always seeing the "Marching 100" in Miami. Like every Florida band kid, I dreamed of being in that band. We grew up immersed in that FAMU precision, sound, energy and musicianship.

From junior year to after high school graduation, I was torn between choosing a college in-state or out of state. I was also considering a military academy. My family did not have any money for me to attend college. I did not even know what I wanted to major in or what I wanted to do with my life. I had great options. Probably too many. I wanted to be an engineer/pilot/astronaut with military background at one point. None of my priorities or ideas included band or majoring in music. I did not even apply to FAMU, running from the "band" stigma that I had earned in high school after attaining all of the highest bandsman awards in Dade County. Classmates who were going to other universities outside of Florida called FAMU "The 13th Grade" since so many graduates enrolled there annually. I fought the FAMU band itch and stigma. However, running from it did not save me!

I soon found myself in that number! I applied to FAMU at the last minute in the summer, and I was admitted when I arrived at pre-drill. My parents dropped me off in Tallahassee, and I headed straight to the band room on my bike with my saxophone strapped on my back in a Tuxedo case. I played the oboe in concert band throughout high school, and I was a drum major at Miami Norland Senior High school. I had not played saxophone in three years. I would have to learn all of the music in the packet in a short time.

Expectations were high in the "Hundred," and there was no shamming. The competition was fierce. Everyone was a drum major, section leader, all-state, all everything, or the "who's who" from where they came. Contrary to the most ignorant thing that I have heard about my band over the years of it being so large that folks slipped through the cracks, everyone could play their horns well! As a reference, many of my freshman brothers and sisters are currently prominent professional musicians, scholars and educators. One of them currently plays with Wynton Marsalis and the Jazz at Lincoln Center Orchestra.

I persevered. My freshman year was as challenging as it was epic. Practices in the FAMU band were performances. Hundreds of spectators attended rehearsals daily and sat on benches to watch. Every "Take it again," you had to bring it! There was never a time to sham or half-a**in practice! Perfect practice for perfect performance. As a freshman, I wanted to try out for drum major, so I worked hard on and off the field. The upperclassmen and drum majors noticed. One evening at the end of the season, I worked so hard that I dislocated my entire patella and leg in practice. I was carted off the practice field in an ambulance. I did not think about the pain or how loud and gruesome the injury was. I was concerned about finishing the last three games of the season, which were the most important to me: homecoming, Miami, and Tampa against Bethune Cookman. I remained on crutches and walked with a cane for a while. I did not recover in time. Even worse, drum major tryouts were that fall.

I would try out anyway, with a leg brace and a cane. I persevered.

I was announced as a FAMU drum major my sophomore year. I learned to lead my peers by example. In 2000, I became a college band director with band students who were either my age or older than me. My priceless HBCU band experiences and lessons informed me in my career as a director of bands at two HBCUs. The idea of hard work, dedication and perseverance stays with me, and I instill this mindset to uplift my students. The mentality of never giving up and finding a focus, regardless of the controversy or confusion that I gained would have never been mastered had I not marched in FAMU's band. I met my wife Aja in FAMU's band, and we instill excellence in our children. Always believe that excuses are obstacles to achievement and build barriers to success. Never let money, pain or any circumstances prevent you from reaching your goal.

About Dr. Jorim & Aja Reid

Dr. Jorim and Aja Reid met on the Highest of Seven Hills at Florida Agricultural & Mechanical University as members of the Incomparable FAMU Marching 100.

While in the band, Aja played BFlat Clarinet, Bass Clarinet in symphonic band, and served as Freshman Class Parliamentarian, 1st Female Song Leader and Band Business Manager. She was Miss Kappa Kappa Psi National Honorary Band Fraternity (98-99), Miss Alpha Phi Omega National Service Fraternity (99-00), and a Beta Phi Chapter member of Tau Beta Sigma National Honorary Band Sorority where she served as Song Leader and Vice President. Mrs. Reid earned a Bachelor's Degree in Business Administration from the FAMU School of Business & Industry and when she was not on the band field, modeled with Epicurean! Fashion Experience. She also has two Masters of Science degrees in Organizational Leadership & Effectiveness and Human Resources Management from Troy State University.

Aja Reid has been in the Human Resources field for over 15 years, serving in positions of impact and leadership in the Hospitality, Logistics, Higher Education, Healthcare, Biotech and Non-Profit industries. She also holds a Senior in Professional Human Resources (SPHR) certification from the Human Resources Certification Institute; a Targeted Selection Interviewer certification from Development Dimensions International; and a North Carolina Public Employment Law certification from the University of North Carolina at Chapel Hill.

Mrs. Reid is the owner of Reid Creative Solutions LLC where she provides HR consulting and training services for small businesses and individuals. Aja enjoys serving her community and volunteers with the Durham Rescue Mission, Book Harvest and Dress-for-Success. She is also a proud member of the Western Wake Chapter of Delta Sigma Theta Sorority Incorporated.

Dr. Jorim Reid served as Head Drum Major in the FAMU Marching 100 and principal Oboist in the Wind Ensemble. He is also a member of the Delta Iota Chapter of Kappa Kappa Psi National Honorary Band Fraternity and a charter member of the Omicron Gamma Chapter of Phi Mu Alpha Sinfonia. Reid is also active with the Beta Phi chapter of Omega Psi Phi Fraternity Incorporated. Jorim graduated from FAMU with a Bachelor's degree in Music Education, received a Master's degree in Music Education from Florida State University and a Doctorate of Musical Arts degree from Boston University.

Dr. Reid is currently the Director of Bands at Fayetteville State University. Since 2000, he has conducted and developed distinctive sound and quality for multiple ensembles at several universities, and received accolades in several competitions and presentations. For 15 years, Reid served as a faculty member, music instructor, arranger, and Band Director at North Carolina Central University (NCCU) in Durham, North Carolina. While there, he reestablished the symphonic bands. In 2004, he created his passion, the Wind Symphony and Concert Bands, to challenge the exceptional musicians within his program and serve as a development group, respectively. Although his first rehearsal in 2001 consisted of only sixteen winds and sweat-suits for uniforms, the band grew to just shy of 150 by 2004.

Under his leadership, the NCCU Marching and Symphonic bands flourished and provided a source of pride and respect for the university, including participating in and winning the honor of being selected to perform in the Honda Battle of Bands six times in the categories of CIAA and Independent Class (2005-2010). Reid has been featured in the publication, Halftime Magazine International, highlighting his patented "Hybrid" marching concept. This approach was forged to play down deficiencies in student musicianship and limited resources and meld traditional and corps styles, resulting in unlimited musical maneuvering and creativity options that enhance the band's performance. This concept is beginning to be imitated, proving Reid's creative work has been the catalyst generating more than 100 million impressions in print, online, and on television. His commitment awarded the NCCU Marching Sound Machine an invitation to the 2011 Tournament of Roses Parade in Pasadena, California.

While at Fayetteville State University, he re-chartered the Theta Tau Chapter of Kappa Kappa Psi National Honorary Band Fraternity and the Theta Alpha Chapter of Tau Beta Sigma National Honorary Band Sorority. Since his arrival to Fayetteville State University, ESPN/The Undefeated HBCU Band Rankings placed the Marching Bronco eXpress (MBX) as Band of the Year for 2017-18, and the number One Division II Band for the 2018-19 season. Reid also presented the high honor of the National Alumni Award from the Fayetteville State National Alumni Association. Dr. Reid is also the owner of Vision Tree LLC, a media production and publishing company.

Jorim and Aja reside in Durham, NC and are the proud parents of Teddy, Aria and Jorim Jr. (JJ).

LaToya Brooks

Forever to Be a Mighty Marching Panther

LaToya Brooks

Clark Atlanta University

My band journey started with a plastic Bundy clarinet that had been passed down from a family friend. Even though it was on its last leg by the time it got to me, I made it work. My family is very musically inclined. We all sing, and my grandmother (R.I.P.) made everybody take piano lessons since she was an organist. Surprisingly though, I was the first one to be in the band. In third grade at Continental Colony ES, I began my "band career". My love for band in secondary school was almost as strong as my love for my family. My band directors became father figures and my bandmates, siblings. My middle and high school directors eventually became mentors. My college band director is the godfather of my child. Some of my closest friends now are people I marched with in band. The band was, and still is, my family.

Upon graduating from the illustrious B.E. Mays High School in Atlanta, I knew I wanted to march in an HBCU band for a few reasons:

1. My high school experience was HBCU-inspired. Our arrangements, marching style and elements, stand chants, and more, mirrored that of Morris Brown, Southern and, my alma mater, Clark Atlanta University.
2. As a student at Mays, we were afforded the opportunity to attend and perform at HBCU homecomings. It was a life changing experience. The most memorable homecoming was North Carolina A&T. I am quite sure I chanted "Aggie Pride!" for at least a week after we left.
3. My band directors, or band dads, went to HBCUs. So, the experience was ingrained in every aspect of my musical journey.

My only challenge was deciding which one I wanted to attend. One thing I *loved*, and still love to this day, is the fact that several HBCU directors held their scholarship auditions at various high schools. I understand now, as a former director, that this is partially for recruitment purposes. However, as a student, it made me feel like somebody genuinely wanted me to attend their institution. While I had multiple scholarship offers, Clark Atlanta made sure I had no choice, but to be a Mighty Marching Panther. I was completely sold on the idea of being able to attend college for free just to play my instrument.

In the summer of 1998, band for me began weeks before school started. We call it Pre-Drill. The band stayed in an apartment-style dorm on campus, and we were expected to be in the band room by 5 a.m. each day. I wasn't used to this concept, as "band camp" in high school started around 9 a.m., at the earliest 8 a.m. While it was a challenge, we had to make it happen. No excuses were allowed because they are tools of incompetence. We'd start bright and early; well, it wasn't bright at 5 a.m. but so goes the saying. Marching fundamentals and workout in the morning, march to the café for breakfast, back to the band room for music rehearsal/sectionals, march to lunch, back for more music, march to dinner, back outside to close the day with more marching. I'm tired just thinking about the level of intensity we had to give daily. Some called it insane. The result was nothing short of amazing, so it was well worth it. By the end of Pre-Drill, we were in the best shape of our lives. We had a book of at least forty to fifty songs, so our 5th quarters lasted until they kicked us out of the stadium.

Pre-drill was not designed just to teach marching and music. We bonded during this time, as well. We spent hours upon hours with people every day, so we were bound to form a bond. This was necessary to be able to work together and become familiar with the people we had to march with. There were opportunities to spend time outside of practice, as well. Band parties, bus rides, buffet-style restaurants…these were the moments that allowed us to become family.

As a freshman, I was immediately introduced to my first set of life lessons that would follow me throughout adulthood:

Lesson #1: **To be early is to be on time. To be on time is to be late. To be late is to PUSH**. Yes, push as in *push-ups*. I'm quite sure in my first year alone, I did at least 5,693 push-ups. I digress. Now, as an adult, I try to get to my destination at least fifteen minutes early. It's a sign of respect. By being there early, I'm respecting your time. In return, my time should be respected. It's also an opportunity for me to be prepared. If we're starting at 5 p.m., I can't walk in the door at that time.

Lesson #2: **Put *everything* in writing and save your receipts**. Before the convenience of handling business online, we were forced to stand in outrageously long lines to be enrolled each semester or to add/drop classes. There were often discrepancies in the information we had versus what the school had. It was imperative that you kept *every* document *or* get everything in writing. I remember our assistant director, Mr. Camp (RIP) putting sticky notes all over his desk and office wall to ensure he remembered everything. He also made us sign for anything he gave us, so we couldn't say we didn't receive it. If we got a stipend for McDonald's, you are signing for that $7. If we got band caps, even ones that you could keep, they had a special numeric system. If you left it laying around the band room, he knew exactly who to address. As a Music Educator, I made sure to use this method as well. Having accurate records has saved me on multiple occasions.

Lesson #3: **Time Management**. While this is a lesson I am still trying to master, I've had an abundance of practice. As a music major, I had to juggle more classes than the average student. Most music classes were only a credit or two, while classes for other majors were at least three or four. So, with a full-time schedule of at least ten classes a semester, Band and Jazz Orchestra included, individual practice time for multiple instruments, away games and performances *and* trying to squeeze in meals, I had to be exceptionally good at time management in order to be successful. As a wife, mother of three, full-time music educator, and "momager to professional performers, there was no time for excuses. I had to get it done. My experience at CAU, specifically as a band student, has been a major help in this area of my life.

I spent four more years learning and growing with the CAU band program. Sophomore year was truly a year of growth - not just for me - but for the band program, as well. We saw an influx of freshmen who jumped at the chance to work under the infamous Cedric Young, who previously served as a high school band director in Atlanta. Joining the CAU band family in 1998 as well, he immediately hit the ground running to continue the longstanding legacy of excellence. Mr. Young played an integral part in my journey to become an educator. He is intelligent, talented, relentless, and unapologetic in his methods for making his band the BEST band. He, like most of my band directors, genuinely cared about me as an individual and as a musician. My well-being was top priority, then band. The lessons I've learned from him have shaped who I am as a person and as an educator. I am grateful to have him in my corner.

My junior year was our "best kept secret" year. We were often slept on because we never really had the opportunity to see bands outside of the SIAC. Eventually, the invitations to battles and performances outside of our normal audience came in. 2001, my fourth year as a Marching Panther, was such a great year for HBCU bands, in general. Every band we saw that year had a great sound, dope shows and creative dance routines. CAU was no different. The most memorable event from that year was having Alabama State University (ASU) on our schedule. We typically prepared for every performance like it was the Super Bowl of band events, but when we faced ASU, it was intense. Our entire band staff at the time were

ASU alums, so it was personal. Practices were longer. Our song book evolved. Even the pettiness surfaced. It was by far one of the best games I've participated in. By then, I was a baritone player, who had just mastered a Bb above the staff, so I was in rare form. I still sing ASU's French horn countermelody from "The Way" to this day.

Then, there was "Drumline". The CAU band had the honor of serving as part of the fictitious Atlanta A&T band in the film. Some band members were also asked to serve as extras in non-band scenes. You can see me dancing right next to Nick Cannon at the party. This was also a pivotal year for the program. We had even more opportunities to see and perform for programs and audiences we typically wouldn't have. As a graduating senior, I experienced one of the most unforgettable years at CAU. In addition to seeing myself on the big screen, I had the honor of participating in the first annual Honda Battle of the Bands, and I was also appointed as drum major in 2002. It was truly an honor to be selected to serve in this position, especially at a time when female DMs were scarce. My band experience was officially complete. Knowing that I was a part of the CAU band legacy is something I will always cherish.

Being in an HBCU band is more than just an extracurricular activity, a scholarship or a free ticket into the games. It's history and tradition, life lessons and an immediate family. It's an experience that provides an unexplainable feeling of pride and power that you carry for a lifetime.

Forever to be a Mighty Marching Panther…

About LaToya Brooks

LaToya Brooks is a native of Atlanta, GA, where she has served as a certified Performing Arts Educator with 20+ years of experience working with and coaching youth and young adults. She earned a B.A. in Music from Clark Atlanta University and an M.S. in Music Education from Tennessee State University. As an undergrad student at CAU, she served as Clarinet Section Leader, Drum Major and Student Director of the Mighty Marching Panther Band. While at TSU, she served as a Graduate Assistant for the Aristocrat of Bands.

LaToya has taught multiple disciplines, from band to chorus to drama, on every level. She served as Assistant Director of Bands at CAU for years before moving to high school band. Her band programs have earned superior ratings in Large Group Performance Evaluations, as well as Solo and Ensemble Festivals. She has served as a Department Chair and has consistently been rewarded for her stellar work in the field.

LaToya currently serves as "mom"ager of 3 amazing daughters who, through her leadership, have experienced success in the entertainment industry. Her background in Performing Arts has allowed her to manage and coach her daughters' careers, resulting in their participation in numerous roles in award winning films, a Netflix series, and, currently, a series regular on a Nickelodeon show. All of these experiences have granted her the opportunity to create her own business, The Brooks Arts Collective. BAC is a company dedicated to serving youth and young adults as it relates to the Arts. Through her business, LaToya created the STEPS TO STARDOM course for parents who desire to get their kids in the TV/Film industry as well.

You can find LaToya in her hometown of Atlanta. In her free time, she enjoys watching movies and spending quality time with her husband, Adam, and their girls, Aria, Skylar and Kai. LaToya prides herself on the relationship she has with God and her commitment to spiritual growth has tremendously helped her navigate through life.

Ebony Burroughs

Who Would I Be Without the BGMM?
Ebony Burroughs
North Carolina A&T State University

I come from a family who loves marching bands. My mother played clarinet and, eventually, became head majorette at Hillside High School in Durham, North Carolina. My father, who had never played an instrument in his life, tried out for drum major to impress my mother. My baby sister, Jessica, eventually followed in our footsteps at this same high school. I grew up in Durham, at a time when the Hillside Marching Hornets constantly tried to out march, out play, and outperform North Carolina Central University, the HBCU up the street. By the time I was a student at Hillside, we were competing with Central during their homecoming parades for the largest crowds. I did not enjoy high school, but the marching band was the saving grace of those days.

We respected Central's band program, but we were in awe of marching bands we rarely got to see up close. Before there was YouTube, we traded VHS tapes, watching field shows, stand battles, and section punches of other HBCU bands. We watched FAMU, Howard, Grambling, Norfolk State, and North Carolina A&T's Blue and Gold Marching Machine, also known as "The small band with the big sound". So many Hillside alums had gone on to join The Marching Machine. Anthony Criss, one of A&T's most electrifying drum majors, was a Hillside graduate. So, when the time came for me to decide where I would be attending college (and just as important, which HBCU band program I would be joining), choosing A&T was a no brainer.

I marched for two years at A&T. I like to think that my participation was notable, since many of my bandmates remember me being there for four years. My first day at band camp, I was terrified. I was a flute player since middle school, and until that first day, I felt I was a solid musician. This was my first experience with imposter syndrome. I was surrounded by talented musicians, some of whom came from performing arts high schools, who played multiple instruments, and were members of high school programs that could compete easily at the collegiate level. They were all out impressive. I wasn't sure I was good enough and, at times, I struggled with managing that insecurity. Still, I knew I would regret not sticking it out, at least to make it to that very first halftime.

I was a shy, late-blooming, awkward, freshman flute player, but to march at A&T, I needed to figure out how to overcome my fear. On occasion, I was chastised by my section leader for failing to have my music memorized or general lapses in excellence. However, nothing was more frightening than the time Dr. Hodge, affectionately known as Doc, pointed to me and commanded me to, "Play!" I don't remember the song, but it was something challenging. The last thing I wanted to do was flub a note or articulation in front of the whole band, within the sacred walls of the band room, in front of *thee* Dr. Johnny B. Hodge, Jr. Considering I do not suffer any PTSD symptoms remembering that event, I must have performed fairly well. Others, however, would not have the same outcome. There is no embarrassment like the cut one would receive from Doc after a poor showing during practice. I quickly learned that the anecdote for my fear of failing and quieting the voice in my head challenging my belonging, was to always be prepared.

For me, being a band member gave me a certain amount of hubris, which was like a B-12 shot for someone like me, who struggled with insecurity. I was a member of the largest organization on campus. We ate lunch together in the cafeteria, even off season. We found each other at parties and in classes. We knew each other walking across the yard, which meant a lot as freshmen. When other first years were still getting their bearings on day one of classes, I had an arsenal of new friends after spending the latter part of the summer preparing for the marching season. Not only did I know who they were; They knew me and acknowledged me when we crossed paths. My band family was my very first network, introducing me to knowledge, experiences and perspectives that still matter to me today. And performing in that first halftime show was worth every ache and discomfort earned from perfecting the craft.

My grades suffered my sophomore year. While I was never a straight A student, I had never been on academic probation, so this left me with a difficult choice. I decided to sit out for a year to concentrate on my studies, not realizing the last year I marched was the final year. I had a brief conversation with Doc, letting him know that I had to put all my energy into graduating on time, which meant taking a heavier course load. I was heartbroken, but he encouraged me.

He said, "You gotta handle your business." He also let me know that I had a place in his band when I was ready to return. That whole marching season, I had so much anxiety, feeling like I was running late to a rehearsal I was no longer expected to attend. To be early is to be on time... I still went to the cafeteria for dinner to fellowship with fellow bands people. Afterward, I walked with them to Frazier Hall, often lingering just outside of the band room. I watched them go through the pre-rehearsal routine of wetting reeds, oiling slides and valves, or simply wrapping up the chatter which began in the caf'. Over time, I stopped walking the full distance, creating some separation between me and the culture I loved. I regretted my decision, but not because it was the wrong thing to do.

Today, I have been out of the band for over twenty years. I now coach software development teams and organizational leaders as Information Technology professional, and yes, I still love HBCU bands. I play music in my home and find myself marching in place, directing, or yelling, "One! Three! Five! Seven!" as I march across the floor to imaginary yard lines. I have not played my flute in at least fifteen years, although I still have it safely tucked away on a bookshelf with sheet music from my band days. In my work, servant-leadership is the primary philosophy. Servant-leaders are focused on the success of the community and committed to the growth of the people in the community. Marching band culture nurtured this philosophy in me. Being a band member meant I was only as good as the person next to me. If one of us was out of step or out of tune, the rest of us might as well have been, too.

HBCU bandsman-ship requires passion. To do this work well, you have to be willing to give up some of the perks of being an average college student. We play tired, sick, bruised, and sometimes bleeding—all because we love what we do. The majority of us will not go on to be professional musicians, band teachers or directors. Maybe we will relive our glory days as members of the alumni band. Today, I am passionate about my work, and that passion drives my desire for excellence, continuous learning and a commitment to relentless improvement. I surround myself with other seasoned professionals who I respect, giving me the same sense of being surrounded by mentors I had in my college days.

I cannot imagine who I would be without my band experience. Would I be a woman who struggles with voicelessness in a profession dominated by men? The Blue and Gold Marching Machine was peppered with young, powerful women, who were full of unapologetic personality. They were not afraid to be seen and heard. My first section leader, Gretta Frie, was one of those women. Would I worry about whether I deserved a seat at tables where decisions were being made? My time in the band validated me as someone who was skilled, capable and influential. I fell in love with band culture, which saved me in high school, then shaped me in college.

Years later, my embouchure is trash. My ability to read music is questionable, at best, and I have likely forgotten the muscle memory for fingering the keys on my flute. I'm certain that the posture for holding my instrument no longer feels natural. Still, in my heart, I am forever a member of the HBCU band tribe, because every part of that experience is present in everything that I do today.

About Ebony Burroughs

Ebony Burroughs is a servant leader, forever learner, and passionate about issues dealing with diversity, inclusion, and equity. Over the last 22 years, Ebony has worked in various roles across industries such as retail, utilities, communications, real estate, finance, and IT consultancy.

Ebony has spent the last 7 years working as an Agile Coach, guiding companies and software development teams through the journey of adopting Agile working practices. Agile is a mindset that prioritizes people-centricity and a commitment to continual improvement, to deliver valuable products and solutions to customers. This mindset and working style is present in everything that Ebony does, including promoting diversity in the profession. In 2020, Ebony Co-founded EBK Syndicate, offering Agile training and certifications. EBK Syndicate partners with Florida A&M University and North Carolina Central University to promote the value of these types of professional certifications to the HBCU community. She has participated in numerous panel discussions and led workshops educating minority professionals about Agile concepts, practices, and professions.

Over the years, Ebony has had to reinvent herself professionally, multiple times in order to advance in her career. Ebony uses her own experience to help others move into careers they feel good about, through her company NexPath Career Coaching, LLC. "Be your own best advocate.", is a common piece of advice she gives clients when preparing for interviews and asking for what they want, whether it is a promotion, a salary increase, or a position more aligned with their passions.

"I never wanted to be an entrepreneur. I only wanted to do work that I cared about and brought me joy." While Ebony may not have aspired to being a "boss", she is a doer, a problem solver, and doesn't shy away from challenges that when met, help positively impact her community. Along with being a small business owner, she actively participates in uncomfortable conversations with her colleagues to improve workplace culture, address the need for allyship, and the responsibilities we have to each other to create a more equitable society.

Ebony graduated from North Carolina A&T State University with a Bachelor of Science in Graphic Communication Systems, returning over a decade later as a distance learner to earn her Master of Science in Information Technology. Over the years she has also earned a host of professional certifications. Ebony is an avid reader, so much so, she joined the North Star Reading Partners Initiative helping children to read at or above grade level by the time they reach the 3rd grade in Charlotte Mecklenburg Schools. She is the oldest of two – her sister Jessica Burroughs, also an A&T graduate – Her mother is a retired IT professional and her father a retired US Army veteran.

Dr. Bridgette Crawford Bell

The Orange and Blue Crush, MSU
Dr. Bridgette Crawford Bell
Morgan State University

I am Bridgette Crawford Bell, a proud alumnus of Morgan State University. The decision to attend college and participate in marching band is one that I did not take likely. The love for all things college football and band was instilled in me from childhood. My dad played football and was in the band while in high school in Alabama. I grew up watching Alabama State, Alabama A&M, Tuskegee, Morgan State, Auburn and, of course, The University of Alabama. On Saturdays, we spent our time watching college football and marching bands.

Our family is originally from a small town in Alabama; however, I grew up in Baltimore. My childhood home, located in northeast Baltimore, was less than five miles from Morgan State University. I cannot truly tell my story without connecting it to my family history. My dad is a Bishop, and for many years, he was the primary organist for our congregations. I loved music since I was a child and wanted to follow in my dad's footsteps.

From the age of eight years old, I learned the piano and the clarinet. During weekdays, my dad drove to the campus of Morgan State University to watch the football team and band practice. To us, watching the band rehearse was just as important as watching the football team practice. We would then leave Morgan, go home, and play marching band around the house. My dad would tap out the Morgan cadence while I marched behind him yelling, "Ayyy Oooo MSU!" This very thing instilled a love in me for the HBCU band culture.

In the 90s, not many HBCU bands received television coverage. The only bands to receive national television exposure were Southern and Grambling at The Bayou Classic. As a high school tuba student, I knew that I wanted to attend an HBCU and major in Music. By senior year, I narrowed my choices down to my number one choice, Grambling. My second choice was Alabama State, and third choice was Morgan. It's safe to say that almost every child wants to move away for college. I was accepted into all three colleges, but soon narrowed my choices down to two. To my surprise, my top two choices were paired to play in a football classic during my senior year. The classic was held at the Old Memorial Stadium in Baltimore on September 17, 1994. I was even more excited about the battle of the bands set to happen the Friday night before the game.

As a senior, I was super excited. I knew this game would be my deciding factor. The day of the Battle of the Bands, I remember excitedly riding to Rash Field to watch. The announcer began as Morgan State Band marched onto the field. To my surprise, this normally small band had a nice boost in numbers. The Morgan State Band's energy was high, and they sounded good.

During the battle of the bands, Morgan played a few stand tunes and completed a field show. The crowd wondered when the guest band would arrive. To our dismay, the guest band never showed up. The next day, I arrived at Memorial Stadium early. I wanted to get an opportunity to meet the other band director. I approached him as the band warmed up, and he assured me that he would be visiting my high school. As I went to find my seat, I could hear an electric familiar sound coming through the tunnel. The Magnificent Marching Machine was chanting, "Ayyyyyy Ooo M-S-U!" with a fire that I'd never heard before. Everyone in the area went scrambling to find the sound. This band was hyped and electrifying.

The Morgan State Band was the smaller band. However, on that day, they packed a mighty punch. I clearly remember watching the much larger guest band take the field. They did their standard dance show. The Morgan State University Magnificent Marching Machine took the field and performed what I now know to be the "L" drill. The quality difference was clear. But if I needed more convincing, their stand performance was superior. The sound of "M3" playing *Follow Me* is clearly branded in my brain until this very day. I was totally sold, but I wanted to still give the other director the benefit of the doubt.

I was prepared to still audition for the band that I considered to be my number one choice. On Monday, September 19, the band director arrived at my high school. He was surprised to see an all-girl, predominately Black show-style band program. As he interviewed me, I explained that I was a tuba player. He gave me a serious side-glance and said, "A little thing like you playing the tuba? How about you try something else if you want to come to my school?"

I said, "No, sir. I am a tuba player."

He said, "You know our tubas are about sixty pounds. Do you think you can handle that?" I proceeded to sit down with my concert tuba and asked if we could continue the audition. I auditioned, but I knew I would no longer pursue that school. After my audition, he was astonished and proceeded to offer me a scholarship. However, I knew Morgan State University was going to be the place for me.

A few months later, Morgan State University invited me to their Fine Arts Day. The faculty performed, the ensembles performed, and I met with the band director. Our conversation was about helping to build a lasting legacy at Morgan State University. I auditioned and the difference was clear. I will always remember the first day of band camp. I received a letter, explaining that band camp registration would begin on a Sunday. Camp was to immediately follow. Nervous and excited, I remembered walking down the hall on that Saturday and seeing a lot of folks in blue, white and gold shirts. They all welcomed me to the band. Their friendly nature and conversation took my nervousness right away. Many recognized me and said, "Hey! You are the girl from the steps." I finally was realizing my dream.

My freshman year was the beginning of a growth period for the Morgan Band program. I was one of four freshman tuba players joining "M3". The first day of band camp began with an orientation.

We met the director of bands and the entire staff. The orientation ended and we soon hit the field. Conditioning and commands always began on Day 1. We had outstanding senior section leadership within the band. My section leader was a female, and she was by far one of the greatest musicians I ever heard. The band members in blue and white kept us motivated. They were the first to run back to position. They marched the hardest and ensured that we were fed throughout the week. I soon found out that the students in blue and white were members of Kappa Kappa Psi National Honorary Band Fraternity and Tau Beta Sigma National Honorary Band Sorority. From the first day, I knew I desired to be a part of Tau Beta Sigma.

During my first year in the band, we had a few home games. But we traveled quite a bit, as well. My first overnight trip was to Woonsocket, Rhode Island. The excitement was clear from the time we loaded the bus. We arrived in this small town and we were treated like celebrities by the African Americans in the community. Overnight trips with the Morgan State Band always meant good, clean fun! Pillow fights and hide and seek in the hotel were a must! We were family from the beginning.

On the yard, the band was a tight-knit community. You could always identify band members because we traveled in packs and we wore our electric blue band jackets. The Morgan State campus loved our band. The highlight of my time at Morgan was the fall of 1997 when I joined Tau Beta Sigma National Honorary Band Sorority. My Epsilon Omega chapter was the top chapter in the country the year I was initiated. Through the sorority, I learned leadership, organization, friendship, sisterhood and endurance. Tau Beta Sigma made me into the woman I am today.

I was honored to serve our band program as the student assistant from 1996 to 1999. I was the band administrator and student leader. I had the honor of creating and implementing many of the organizational tools and some of the "M3" paraphernalia still used today.

After graduating, I was hired as the assistant to the director of bands. I am the first female to work as a non-auxiliary assistant band staff member. During my time, I had the opportunity handle the various business aspects of the band program, including establishing the band travel itineraries, attending various athletic meetings, adjudicating band competitions, conducting the Magnificent Marching Machine, Symphonic and Pep Band. I attribute who I am as band director, music department chair and teacher specialist to the training I received from the Director of Bands, Melvin Miles, Jr., and the Morgan State University Band program.

About Dr. Bridgette Crawford Bell

Dr. Bridgette Crawford Bell is a Director of Band and Teacher Specialist for School Performance and Achievement in Harford County, Maryland. Bridgette is also the co-host of *The Marching Podcast*.

Bridgette, grew up in Baltimore, Maryland. She received her Bachelor of Arts (1999) and Masters of Art degrees (2005) in Music Education/Conducting from Morgan State University. While matriculating at Morgan State University, she played the tuba in the Magnificent Marching Machine "M3" Band, Pep Band, and Symphonic band. Bridgette was the tuba section leader and served as the student assistant to the director of bands from 1996 – 1999.

After graduating, Bridgette joined the Morgan State Band Staff as the Assistant to the Director of Bands from 1999 – 2012. In 1999, she also began her career as a music teacher in the Harford County School System. Bridgette has worked for the Harford County Public for the past 22 years and has taught band, orchestra and chorus. Her ensembles have received local, state and, national recognition for outstanding musicianship. Bridgette is currently a teacher specialist for school performance and achievement. In addition to her current role, Bridgette teaches graduate courses and serves a curriculum writer for the Maryland State Department of Education. She has been involved in educational and music leadership for 20+ years. Bridgette has served as department chair, adjudicator, workshop leader, clinician and private/applied instructor. She is also a trusted professional consultant for the National Teacher Board Certification for music standards.

Bridgette is a member of Tau Beta Sigma National Honorary Band Sorority (Fall 1997), Alpha Kappa Mu Honor Society (1998), Delta Sigma Theta Sorority Inc. (Spring, 2007), the National Education Association, Maryland Music Educator Association, HBCU Band Director Consortium, and the Association of Black Woman Band Directors (Director of Membership).

Davon Bagley

From Band Camp to Hollywood: My'hBCU Band Experience

Davon Bagley

Bethune-Cookman University

"Ahh BCC, Ahh BCC Wildcats! Give me some slack cause if you don't, I won't scratch your back. But if you do, I swear I'll march for you… the Marching Cats! That's where it's at. We got soul, so let's go!"

Those words molded me into the man I am today.

It was the fall of 1998, one of the most terrifying, yet exciting times I can remember. I was leaving my small hometown in Virginia, headed to Bethune-Cookman College in Daytona Beach, Florida, a foreign city that was hundreds of miles away from home. Was I ready emotionally? Nope! The truth is, I was a *wreck*. I did not know if I had made the right decision in leaving home and going so far away to college. I knew I was a good trumpet player. I never questioned my skills and ability. I kept saying to myself, "Mr. Wells must see something in me to give me a full scholarship to play in his band. I have to go." It also helped that Mr. Wells was my middle school music teacher years prior. I already knew him. I already knew what I was getting myself into. *Kind of.* But it still did not shake the fear of the unknown.

The time had finally come for me to pack my things and say, "Goodbye" to my family and friends. I remember the day like it was yesterday. All my friends and family had come to my house to send me off. I cried a like a baby. I knew it would be months before I would see anyone again. But there was no turning back at this point.

"B-CC, here I come!"

When I made it to Daytona Beach, and I saw the Bethune-Cookman College sign, suddenly, I was excited to be there. There were four other classmates from my high school who were also awarded the same scholarship. So, I was in good company. My roommate was my friend from home, which made me more comfortable. When we attended freshman orientation, Mr. Wells told our parents that it was not going to be easy. It was going to be hard. He also told our parents that we would be calling home, ready to quit. But I was no quitter. I was up for the task. *So I thought.*

My first day of band camp as a freshman, I was up at 6 a.m. to be at band practice by 6:45 sharp for breakfast. What they called band camp, I called boot camp! All the freshmen lined up in parade formation every morning, marching through the middle of campus to get to the cafeteria for breakfast. Our non-band peers were not fans of us waking them up every morning, chanting; "Ahh BCC, Ahh BCC Wildcats!" near their windows. This is also what introduced me to discipline and the importance of time management.

As much as I thought I was prepared to march in an HBCU band because of the greatness of my high school band program, I was not *truly* ready for what was to come. The early morning report times, the long hours of band practice, the militant-style sectionals—all in preparation for a "football game"—became a little too much for me. I never told anyone this but, my second week of band camp, I sent an e-mail to the band director at Norfolk State University. I told him I was interested in transferring and becoming a part of the Spartan Legion. He welcomed me with open arms and offered me a scholarship. I didn't think the experience would have been any easier, but I would have at least been back home with my family. Obviously, I did not take him up on his offer. Eventually, I got it together and enjoyed my time in Bethune-Cookman's band.

Besides, the sheer power, musical maturity and disciplined stature of the program was nothing short of amazing. What Mr. Wells was able to accomplish in only his second year as head band director at the time was astonishing. I was proud to be a member of what would eventually become a household name in not just the HBCU band world, but the band world in its entirety.

The one special thing I can say about being in the band at B-CC is that we prepared for each performance like it was our Super Bowl. We did not practice extra hard based on what band we were seeing across the field from us on any given week. We practiced being the best we could be, without compromise. I took this energy with me into the real world. One performance was the exception: The Florida Classic! The biggest game of the season against the world-famed Florida A&M University Marching 100! Not only was I excited to finally see the band I had heard about for so many years *live*, but it would be the end of my freshman experience in the band. No more marching to the cafeteria early in the morning and no more white t-shirts! Aside from graduating from high school with honors, completing my first season in B-CC's band was one of my greatest accomplishments.

To this day, I tell people that being a part of B-CC's band had the biggest impact on me as a man. It had groomed me in unimaginable ways. I became a leader. I was pushed to be better in the classroom and in life, not just in the band room. I was afforded the opportunity to travel to places in and outside of the country. My first international trip was traveling to Nassau, Bahamas for a football game against Morgan State. Albeit I was bitten up by red ants during the halftime show and had bumps everywhere. The experience was one I would never forget.

During my years in the band, it became extremely popular. Our band was a household name. We were getting calls from big corporations, the Daytona 500, NFL teams and other mainstream outlets. Everyone wanted to work with Bethune-Cookman's band. In fact, in 2001, during my junior year, Hollywood came knocking with an invitation for the band to be a part of the movie, "Drumline." All the hard work and dedication we had put in manifested this amazing opportunity. When we received word that we were traveling to Atlanta to be a part of the movie, we were ecstatic. It was even more exciting for me because my dream was to work in entertainment. However, I had no clue where to start. I just wanted to be on a movie set and see the inner workings (and obviously hear my mom and dad brag that their baby was in "Drumline").

Being a member of the band automatically made me a cool kid on campus. Honestly, we were more popular than the football team and any other organization on campus. We were well respected, and many people looked up to us. We were the heart and soul of the school for years.

Although being a part of the best HBCU band was nothing short of amazing, it was time for me to get serious about my next steps after college. I was grateful to Mr. Wells for giving me the opportunity to be a part of greatness for three years. I spoke with him and mentioned that I would not participate my senior year in the band program. There were things I wanted to accomplish as a student that I could not do being a part of the band. I needed to set myself up for success.

The spring semester of my senior year, I took the semester off and took an internship at Walt Disney World for course credit. This was a hard decision because it meant I would graduate a semester later than my peers. But it was something I thought I should do. It ended up being the best decision I could have made. During my internship at Walt Disney World, I visited the BET Soundstage in Downtown Disney on my off days and networked with management. I eventually was offered a security job with BET Soundstage part-time upon completion of my internship. I made the drive from Daytona Beach to Orlando, which was over an hour drive each way, for my shift for quite a few months. The grind eventually paid off. I was introduced to a producer of BET's hit show "Hits from the Streets" for the "Spring Bling" taping, which had been filming in Daytona Beach for the last couple of years. That was the opportunity that I had been waiting for. I was that much closer to my dream of working in entertainment.

When I completed my internship at Disney World, I started as a production assistant for one of the most popular shows on BET. I was on a roll! I still wanted to have the total college experience, though. So, I ran for homecoming king in the fall of 2001, and I won. I will always remember Mr. Wells allowing me the opportunity to campaign in the band room during his practice, even though I'd made the decision not to participate in band my senior year. That is when I knew I had earned his respect. I not only accomplished what

I set out to do while being away from the band my last season, but I received a call from the same producer who hired me as a production assistant to go to Washington, D.C. After graduation, I had the opportunity to work for BET in the Music Specials Department. The dream I had been praying for since high school manifested. The dream that I had no clue how I would accomplish was aligned for me from the first day I stepped foot on campus that hot fall day in 1998. It was destined.

If it were not for Bethune-Cookman College, and the band specifically, I probably wouldn't be where I am today. Being a part of the band taught me so much and shaped my future. I wanted to be the best—not only in the band—but in life. I am grateful and forever indebted for the opportunity to attend Bethune-Cookman. I have made lifelong friends, who I consider family. That experience cannot be taken away from me.

Hail, Wildcats!

About Davon Bagley

Davon Bagley is a 2002 Business Administration graduate of Bethune-Cookman University (formerly Bethune-Cookman College, B-CC), and an alumnus of the famed Marching Wildcat band. A resident of Atlanta, GA via Washington, DC, Davon has made a household name for himself in the entertainment industry. Davon started his career as an intern in the television industry while a student at B-CC As an intern for the popular shows "Hits from the Streets" and "Spring Bling". Upon graduating from B-CC, Davon was offered a full-time position by BET Networks in Washington, DC. He joined the team as a Production Assistant in the Special Projects Department where he quickly moved into the role of Associate Producer for the network's movie specials and the then longest running show in cable history, "Bobby Jones Gospel." Not only was he able to tackle the creative side of television, but he was also able to evolve into Production Management as Production Coordinator and Production Manager on BET's highly rated tentpole shows (BET Awards, Soul Train Awards, Hip Hop Awards, and Celebration of Gospel) among others. While working full time in his new career, Davon wanted more and saw the need to further his education beyond his bachelor's degree. In 2006, he earned his MBA from Troy University and set out to follow his dream of starting his very own entertainment company, Vonlee Entertainment, that focuses on celebrity bookings, event planning, and road management services for Fortune 500 companies and some of the biggest names in music and film. Davon continues to flourish in his career as he has played an integral role in various productions to include Netflix's Emmy nominated "Love Is Blind," "Rickey Smiley for Real," "Married At First Sight," the "Real Housewives" franchise and countless other popular shows in Production Management. He is currently the Creative Set Executive for the scripted shows, "Boomerang," "Bigger," and "First Wives Club." A follower of all things HBCU, he and his best friend came together to create "A Different World LIVE," an organization that travels around the country uniting HBCU Alumni, Black Greek Letter Organizations (BGLO), and lovers of the culture. Davon, a member of Kappa Alpha Psi Fraternity, Incorporated, is a testament to their motto, "Achievement in Every Field of Human Endeavor".

D. Rashad Watters

The Elite. The Untouchable. The Hampton University Marching Force!

D. Rashad Watters

Hampton University

"The supreme manifestation of all that is precision. The epitome of excellence. The elite. The untouchable. The Hampton University Marching Force! Hit 'em with that wall of sound!"

This was the mantra exclaimed by the announcer for Hampton University's incredible marching band before every performance.

I was proud to be a part of that number. But to understand what the Hampton University's "Marching Force" meant to me, and thousands of others, let's take a trip into my past.

Like many African Americans, I was a part of a church with a great music department. At Peace Missionary Baptist Church, I grew up hearing my parent's choir, "The Voices of Peace" lift their voices to praise God. It was melodious, soulful and beautiful. It was loud!

I learned that, when singing your praises to God, you sing with all the air in the lungs that God gave you. Was there any doubt then that after I started expressing myself with a wind instrument like the trombone, I would want to play the very same way? I played loud with everything I had.

That didn't transfer very well into mainstream music education. I was continually scolded for playing out of balance and being too loud. Criticism came not just from my teachers, but also my peers. But I was only expressing myself the way I had been taught—with all the energy and passion I had.

There was more. My church upbringing taught me to memorize music immediately. Other than congregational hymns, we *never* used sheet music in practice, and certainly not in performances. Memorizing was a natural part of life for me.

But, in mainstream band programs, using sheet music in performance is acceptable. My peers used music lyres. These are music holders that can be attached to an instrument so that players can use their sheet music *in performance*. It turns my stomach just to type that.

My separation from my peers went even further. In church, the choirs I performed with sang different songs each Sunday and had an extensive catalogue to choose from.

In my high school marching band, on the other hand, we performed the same music all season. We often started the season by performing the first song of our show, then adding the other three or four songs as the year progressed.

I was also separated from the mainstream musical environment in one other way. This one came not because of my background in church, but from a few of my peers in my high school band. When I joined the band, there were several Black males in the program who would not only play the music assigned to them, but they also learned popular songs from the radio and performed them at our football games. These young men soon graduated from high school, but I continued to carry on their legacy by striving to get bandmembers to learn popular music, as well.

To his credit, our band director was cool about small groups of instrumentalists working together to play popular music. But that was never really a part of the full band program's training.

I don't blame my mainstream music teachers. They just taught me what they knew to be right. I just knew that it wasn't right *for me*.

I needed something different. I just didn't know what it was yet.

My father introduced me to HBCU band culture by showing me Southern University's Human Jukebox on TV and by encouraging me to go to Florida A&M University's High School Band Camp. Later, I saw North Carolina A&T University's band in person. I knew there was more to life than what I had been exposed to previously.

That's when it all changed.

In August of 1995, I enrolled at Hampton University in Hampton, Virginia. I went there because they had a Music Engineering major, and they had an HBCU marching band.

As a part of the Hampton University "Marching Force", my life went in a completely different direction.

No longer did my passionate, loud playing make me the source of ostracism. Instead, Hampton's director, Barney Smart, helped me refine that power. Instead of just being loud, my sound became bold and full. Mr. Smart took the explosive sound of many young instrumentalists from across the nation, and the world, to create what he called the "Wall of Sound."

Gone were the days of looking at my peers sideways because they couldn't, or wouldn't, memorize their music. No lyres were allowed in Hampton's Marching Force, or any HBCU marching band for that matter.

Instead of playing a total of about ten songs a season, like in high school, Hampton's music catalogue was about eighty to 120 songs a season! That excluded dance routines of about four to six songs, which changed weekly, and songs played by my section, the trombone section. The trombone section added another ten songs to that list.

Mr. Smart led us to accomplish all of this, but he did another thing, as well. He taught us not only to have pride in what we could do, but also in being unique. Hampton's band was different, and Mr. Smart taught us to take pride in that.

Our Sound Was Different

Mr. Smart taught me to refine my sound. He didn't just do that for me, though. He taught all of the Hampton bandmembers to play with power right up to the point of distortion, but never crossing that line. While similar marching bands were competing to be the loudest, regardless of sound quality, "The Force" prided itself on sounding the best.

Our Repertoire Was Different

Many bands had several staple songs. "Staples" are to an HBCU band what "standards" are to a jazz band. These are songs that bands play regularly. Common staples in the world of HBCUs are "Skin I'm In" by Cameo and "SOS" by the SOS Band.

Staple songs are usually played when the band is in the stands at a football game. We played just one, "Talking Out the Side of Your Neck" by Cameo. We played it at the start of every game. Other than that, our repertoire was filled with the newest songs on the radio. Mr. Smart never wanted us to be like other bands who played the same songs. He wanted us to have our own unique identity.

Every year, we pushed ourselves to relearn our repertoire, instead of allowing it to grow stale.

This spilled over to our field performances, as well. Almost every single one of our field shows was composed of brand-new music that we had not seen the year before, or even the week before. Even beyond this, Mr. Smart wanted our repertoire to stand out in other ways. If there was a song every band was going to play, we simply would not play it. In 1995, Michael Jackson released his song "You Are Not Alone." As we traveled across the nation performing, almost every opposing band we ran into played this song in their show. We on the other hand, never did. Our band separated ourselves by playing "We Must Be in Love" by singing group Pure Soul, masterfully arranged by assistant band director, Al Davis.

The Difficulty Level of Our Music Was Different

Most bands simplified the rhythms of the song when writing the music down. Some wrote the music in ways that were easier for bands to play. Other bands played arrangements that were focused on making it easy to memorize music. Mr. Smart never had this type of sympathy for us.

Our repertoire was filled with rhythms dictated exactly as the singer sang them, in whatever key the original musician played them in. That was no small feat! Those who know music know that keys that are great for piano and guitar are quite difficult for bands. We excelled anyway!

Our Trombone Section Was Different

Our band staff constantly pushed the whole band, particularly Hampton's trombone section, "Slide-Force." While other trombone sections played long tones behind the other instruments, our band staff constantly gave us the melody, pushing us from the highest notes in our range to our lowest. There were only a few songs during my matriculation at Hampton where we didn't have the melody. Mr. Smart even featured our section on a nationally televised performance.

That televised performance, the 1999 Heritage Bowl against Southern University, was my last performance with Hampton's band. Hampton's band had taken me, and thousands of others, from being musicians who couldn't find their place in the world of music and gave them a home. A place where they could express the musical identities impressed upon them in their youth. Hampton's band molded each of these young people into one unit.

"Into the supreme manifestation of all that is precision. The epitome of excellence. The elite. The untouchable...The Hampton University Marching Force."

About D. Rashad Watters

Rashad is a 2000 graduate of Hampton University in Hampton, VA with a BS Degree in Music Engineering and Technology.

While attending Hampton, Rashad traveled across the country with the "Marching Force" Showstyle marching band where he was vice-president, and assistant trombone section leader. He also performed with Hampton's premier wind ensemble the "Symphonic Winds" as a bass trombonist and was chosen to perform with the Inter-Collegiate Music Association's All-Star Band also as a bass trombonist.

While at Hampton, Rashad became a charter member of Phi Mu Alpha Professional Music Fraternity and served as its first colony vice-president.

Rashad performed a Senior Honors Recital and at his graduation ceremony at Hampton, he was given the high honor of directing the University Band and the assembled congregation in the singing of the university's Alma Mater.

After graduating from Hampton, Rashad attended the University of North Carolina at Greensboro and performed with the university's Trombone Ensemble at the International Trombone Festival in Nashville, TN. During this time, in addition to performing with and arranging for UNCG's pep band, Rashad also performed and arranged with the pep band of North Carolina A&T State University.

During his time at UNCG, Rashad continued to diversify his musical background by traveling, performing, and competing with "Carolina Gold", an independent Senior Drum & Bugle Corp.

Continuing to stay immersed in the culture of Showstyle marching band, Rashad attended marching band performances throughout the nation, and became a renowned commentator on marching bands through his thorough "Prunalysis" performance critiques submitted on websites such as The5thQuarter.com and Bandhead.org.

His detailed and unbiased critiques of the Showstyle artform earned him a recurring spot on the HBCU Marching Band focused, "The 90 Degree Show", as a guest analyst and a host of his own "Prunalysis" show, both on "The Marching Podcast" Network.

Working along with Joe Beard at the Marching Podcast, and Author Dr. Kevin Davenport, Rashad spearheaded the creation of the "The Director Series" video series aimed at helping Showstyle band directors improve in their craft.

In 2011, Rashad founded Block Band Music & Publishing, LLC a company that sells Instruments, equipment and music to marching bands both across the nation and internationally. To date, Block Band has sold well over 1000 musical arrangements and delivered over $100,000 in equipment to marching band programs. Block Band has also hired dozens of arrangers, drill-writers, social media specialists and other staff members, most of which are HBCU graduates in its 10 years of operation.

In addition, Block Band has helped to sponsor Showstyle Marching Band competitions across the nation.

Currently, Rashad resides in Durham, NC where he is CEO of Block Band Music & Publishing, hosts a Video and TV show review channel, "Color Commentary" and is director of the Peace Missionary Baptist Church Male Chorus.

Taylor L. Whitehead

VSU Changed My Life & I'm So Glad

Taylor L. Whitehead

Virginia State University

To my knowledge, the first marching band I ever witnessed was Virginia State College's "Sounds of Distinction" around 1978. I was only five years old, but I was utterly excited to be attending a college homecoming game with my parents, Leonard and Janis Whitehead. I'm not sure what it was, but something on that brisk October day sparked my interest and changed my life forever. Maybe it was the thunderous drumbeat. Perhaps it was the brass section's harmony or the energy and enthusiasm that the band displayed marching into the stadium as the crowd stood to their feet. Nine years later, I found myself playing sousaphone in my high school band. During my junior and senior years, I served as the band's lone drum major. It was during that period that I realized I had a sincere passion for music and, more precisely, marching bands.

As a high school student in the late 80s and early 90s, I looked forward to seeing HBCU band halftime shows on Black Entertainment Television (BET). I must have watched one Jackson State University halftime show over one hundred times. I dreamed of maybe one day being in JSU's "Sonic Boom of the South" and performing on television. While I had several college options, my parents and my high school band director had already declared me a future Trojan. My band director, Dennis Snead, was a graduate of Virginia State University. He always encouraged students to attend his alma mater. He took pride in exposing us to as many opportunities at the institution as possible. Both of my parents were also alumni. They had pretty much decided that I would attend the school they affectionately called "State." While I somehow always felt I probably would end up at VSU, I tried numerous times to convince my parents to send me elsewhere. Because I grew up in rural Meherrin, Virginia, I wanted to live in a metropolitan city more than anything. Nevertheless, as I got closer to graduation, I could tell that my plans weren't working out. I was about to be sporting orange and blue.

During my last semester in high school, VSU's band director, Harold J. Haughton, Sr., personally visited my house to recruit me. Before coming to Virginia State in 1984, he led the 180-member Jackson State University band program. They were one of the top HBCU bands in the nation. Mr. Haughton was considered a legend in the HBCU band world, and I felt honored to have him in my home. As he talked while enjoying the dinner that my father had prepared, he told me about how the VSU band could benefit from my participation. He told me it would significantly impact my life. Throughout our conversation, I tried to give several silly reasons about why I could not attend VSU. I needed to be in the city. However, as the evening progressed, I quickly realized that I was about to talk myself out of something that I would most likely later regret forever. How could I possibly turn this man down? How could I disappoint my parents by not attending their alma mater? I had to start preparing for Petersburg to be my next home.

Three months later, I auditioned and accepted a band scholarship to attend VSU. By then, I couldn't wait to join the same band program I had experienced as a small child. After arriving on campus, I originally planned to major in Communications because I had hoped to become a successful radio disc jockey one day. However, it was Mr. Haughton who inspired me to major in music. He said, "I feel like you will make a hell of a band director one day." While I never had any teaching plans, when Mr. Haughton spoke, people listened. Once again, I took his advice. I immediately walked to the registrar's office and declared Music Education as my major. This decision unquestionably changed my life and shaped me into the man that today most people in the band world refer to as merely "Whitehead."

As a Music major, I enjoyed the benefits of being in a small department where each professor got to know their students personally. As a member of the "Trojan Explosion" Marching Band, I enjoyed some of the best experiences of my life. While traveling up and down the east coast, performing for thousands of fans was always exciting. Being a part of a loving HBCU band family will always be one of the most incredible experiences of my life. It was in that family that I made relationships and bonds that remain to this day. Because our band was not extremely large, almost everyone in the program became quite close. Our band building, Lindsay-Montague Hall, became our home away from home. If we ever wanted to see our extended family, we went there. When practice was over, we refused to leave. We loved being a part of the band, and we loved Virginia State.

Yearly, I looked forward to our halftime battles with the "Spartan Legion" of Norfolk State University, "The Force" of Hampton University, and the "Sound Machine" of North Carolina Central University. I enjoyed the fierce competition versus other bands in the Central Intercollegiate Athletic Association (CIAA). As I think back, I enjoyed college so much that I wish my time there never had to come to an end. My experience at Virginia State undoubtedly prepared me for the future. Under Mr. Haughton's baton, I learned the benefits of discipline, time management, musicianship, showmanship, hard work, dedication and sacrifice. He was strict and firm. But all who came in contact with him understood that he was passionate about his craft and loved his students. I also found this to be the case with many of my professors, other faculty and staff members I encountered on campus. On our campus, which set high above the Appomattox River, it was evident that we, as a student body and campus community, were a family.

During my sophomore year, Mr. Haughton asked me to consider serving as a drum major for the upcoming season. He felt I had strong leadership skills. Even though I decided not to, I still took on a leadership role as a student director. I stayed by Mr. Haughton's side every possible minute. Daily, I listened to his stories about how he had successfully built band programs over the years. I became a sponge and tried to absorb all the knowledge I could. I wanted to carry on his legacy and, hopefully one day, be considered a legend, as well. I can vividly remember sitting in the back of the band room, dreaming of one day returning to VSU as a band director.

After graduating from VSU, I accepted a position as band director at Warren County High School in Warrenton, North Carolina. When I took the job, I had no idea of the struggles I would go through or the many accomplishments that would come years later. One thing I knew for sure, VSU had prepared me to give everything I had to succeed. In my twenty years of leading the WCHS "Dynamic Marching Machine," I led the band to many local, state and national championships. Possibly my most significant achievement was leading the Warren County "Steel Stix" Drumline to nine High Stepping National Drumline Championships. Even though I was responsible for Warren County's band, I always kept close ties to Virginia State and continued to help with the band program, just as the VSU band members helped my high school group. My love for my Virginia State University never changed. I remained a proud and loyal Trojan. I always hoped to return to "The Hill" one day and carry on my director's legacy.

In 2013, I got that opportunity when the newly appointed band director, James Holden, Jr., asked me to serve as his assistant. I had waited years for this call. The chance to return to my beloved alma mater has been an incredible journey over thirty-five years in the making. I'll always be thankful for having such a humbling opportunity. Today, I treat my students with the same level of respect that Mr. Haughton treated us. I try to expose them to as many new opportunities and experiences as possible. Most of all, I try to instill in them the same love for VSU that I've had since I was a child. I often tell them that they may not realize it now, but later in life, they will understand the school's influence on molding them into productive society members.

I can proudly say that my education and experiences at Virginia State University profoundly affected making me who I am today. Without a doubt, VSU changed my life, and I'm so glad.

About Taylor L. Whitehead

Taylor Leonard Whitehead was born in Farmville, Virginia, on April 24, 1973, to Janis and Leonard Whitehead. He attended Central Senior High School in Victoria, Virginia, where he played tuba and also served as the marching band's drum major his junior and senior years. After high school, Taylor attended Virginia State University, where he participated in the VSU "Trojan Explosion" Marching Band. He graduated from Virginia State in 1996 with a Bachelor of Science degree in Music Education and received his Master of Music Education from Norfolk State University in 2008.

In 1997, he accepted the position of Band Director at Warren County High School in Warrenton, North Carolina. Under his leadership, the Warren County High School "Dynamic Marching Machine" became one of the most successful show-style marching bands in North Carolina and throughout the nation. Between 2006 and 2017, the Warren County Band won nine National High Stepping Drumline Championships, seven Class A National High Stepping Band Championships, two National Danceline Championships, two National Auxiliary Championships, five Class A State High Stepping Band Championships, as well as over one hundred 1st Place Drumline Trophies. In 2013, Taylor returned to his alma mater to serve as the Assistant Band Director at Virginia State University on a part-time basis.

In January of 2018, Mr. Whitehead departed Warren County after over 20 years of service to become the full-time Assistant Band Director at Virginia State University. In addition to working with the band program, he is also a member of the music faculty. Mr. Whitehead is very active in several collegiate organizations, including the HBCU Band Directors' Consortium and the Intercollegiate Music Association.

He is a member of Alpha Phi Alpha Fraternity Incorporated, Kappa Kappa Psi National Band Fraternity, Tau Beta Sigma National Honorary Band Service Sorority, Phi Mu Alpha Sinfonia,

Tuba Phi Tuba Brass Fellowship, Mu Phi Sigma National Percussion Fraternity, and Phi Delta Kappa International Association. He has served as President of the North Carolina Show-style Band Director's Association and advisor to the National Board for High Stepping Nationals and the Grand Board for Tuba Phi Tuba Brass Fellowship. In 2010-2011, he was selected as Teacher of the Year for Warren County High School. He was also selected at the SPECTACULAR MAGAZINE "Man of the Year" in Education in 2013.

Taylor currently resides in Chesterfield County, Virginia, and is married to Angelica Whitehead. They have three children, Taylor, Jeremiah, and Trinity.

Charles M. Conner

The Band Chose Me

Charles M. Conner

North Carolina A&T State University
Fayetteville State University

"I didn't choose the band; the band chose me."
– Charles M. Conner

As I reflect on my historically black college and university experience, specifically my HBCU band experience, I must go back to the beginning. I attended my first HBCU football game at Fayetteville State University. One of my high school drum majors and good friends extended an invitation to come to the game with him. I was really excited to attend my first college game, mainly to watch the actual football game. Little did I know that football game would open my eyes up to a whole new world. I entered the stadium and immediately felt the energy. There were so many people, smiling, laughing and enjoying the overall experience.

Upon arrival to my second HBCU game, and my first Aggie Eagle Classic, the forecast predicted heavy rainfall. Nothing was stopping my friends and me from attending that game. We made our way up the highway. I jumped out of the van, whipped out my camcorder, and created my very own band tape. At this point, we decided to split up to cover more ground. Of course, I was on the A&T side of the stadium. This tape is still in my possession today. It contains a young kid singing "Aggie Spirit" and mimicking movements from the band and humming the beats from the drumline. I looked at each member of the band like they were celebrities. Regardless of what anyone else thought, they were to me. This day, I declared I would be a member of the Aggie band one day.

During my senior year, I applied to only HBCUs. I knew in my heart that A&T was the school for me. Before I would get an opportunity to study under Dr. Hodge, and join the Blue and Gold Marching Machine, my path was directed back to my first HBCU band, the Marching Bronco Express at Fayetteville State University. Dr. Harold Bray was the newly appointed band director. FSU was close to home, and financially, all four years of school were paid for if I attended FSU. I grew up in a single-income home for most of my life. So, the decision to attend FSU was a tough one, but a necessary one for my family and myself. After making my decision, I informed my high school band director of where I would attend school the following year. When he asked what I was majoring in, I replied, "Music Education."

His response was, "Finally! You saw the light. I knew it from the start!"

Under the direction of Dr. Harold Bray, the Marching Bronco Express experienced a huge facelift from the previous leadership and history of the program. The band was smaller than my high school band in overall numbers, but not in heart, love and spirit. One of those facelifts included no longer being allowed to play in the drumline due to my primary instrument for my major being the trombone. Even though this was not what I wanted to hear, I was always taught to follow the direction of the band director/coach, whether I agreed with their instruction or not. Dr. Bray had high expectations for all his students. His knowledge and proficiency on his instrument were amazing. He was the first musician I had ever seen or heard execute circular breathing. His approach toward the band and music was extremely focused and intense.

After the completion of the basketball season at FSU, I requested my transcripts, called Dr. Hodge at A&T, and informed my parents that I was transferring in the fall of 2001. I vividly remember the phone conversation with Dr. Hodge.

He said, "Son, you finally ready to come to A&T now?" He asked for my full name, address, intended major, social security number, and told me he would call me the next day.

The next morning, the phone rang at 6 a.m. A stern voice said, "Son, are you still in bed? You should be up practicing if you plan on being a band director."

I immediately knew that he was a man of his word and, secondly, that he played no games! He informed me of my dorm room, class schedule, and the day I would be required to report to band camp. I also learned during this conversation that he would go above and beyond for all of his students.

Upon my arrival at 1601 E. Market Street (North Carolina A&T), I met some of the band members prior to band camp. One of them in particular just so happened to play trombone and major in Music Education, too. He became a constant source of inspiration and motivation. He serves as a mentor even to this day. The word "loyalty" took on a whole different meaning. As a member of the Blue and Gold Marching Machine, family, discipline, and loyalty were instilled in us from day one. A BGMM tradition was the day one "Valley" speech from Dr. Hodge, which immediately informed us who ran the show. My first year as a member of the BGMM was an amazing experience, full of great music, travel, late nights and a sense of pride that was second to none.

That next season was one of the most historic seasons and greatest editions of the BGMM. It was the fall of 2002. I can remember the first ictus (downbeat from the baton/director) during the first rehearsal. The echoes of "Battle Hymn Chorale" still ring in my mind from that day. This was the last season of the BGMM under the direction of Dr. Johnny B. Hodge. Knowing this, it was important that we sent him off on a high note. Our final performance under his direction was against South Carolina State University in Atlanta, which included a Friday night gym battle of the bands and the traditional Saturday college football game. I honestly don't believe the other band understood what was about to happen to them that weekend. We were surely on a mission. There's a historic photo of Dr. Hodge walking off the field, arms raised, and the biggest smile on his face. We knew at that moment that we'd sent him off in true Aggie fashion. It was truly an end of the Dr. Johnny B. Hodge era.

My next three seasons were under the direction of Dr. Kenneth G. Ruff, a fellow Aggie, assistant band director, and former student of Dr. Hodge, as well. This season was full of travel and exposure at different band events. Throughout my time under the leadership of Dr. Ruff, I learned a lot about leadership, organization and the characteristics needed to build a successful program. In 2003, we were blessed with an opportunity to travel to Las Vegas for the Las Vegas Classic vs. Southern University. Not only was this a great travel experience due to a large majority of the band never visiting Las Vegas, let alone having flown on a plane before, but we also got to face head up versus another storied band program. The start of the season was amazing, to say the least. This was the largest band in the history of the A&T band, with the number of members totaling 245 to 260 at one point. This was the largest section I had an opportunity to play with, which included twenty-seven trombones. From the start, the "old-heads" knew that change was not coming. It was *here*.

Some of the change was met with disagreement. But changes were necessary for the band to progress and grow into what the BGMM is today. The season started off with a first-place win at the first Defeat the Beat Battle of the Bands, with a $25,000 prize, as well. This was the first performance under the direction of Dr. Ruff, which I believe helped usher in the new era of the BGMM. As the next few seasons rolled along, different expectations, traditions and leadership training were established to not only build the band, but the overall college student.

The fall of 2005 was my last season as a member of the BGMM, but not as an HBCU band member, unbeknownst to me. I was officially a super senior, ready to graduate, and complete my journey in the ranks for my last "hoo-ra". This season was probably the most difficult for me in terms of physical ability and overall growth. I was appointed section leader for the baritone section. In November of 2005, my family and I were hit with a major blow. The overall health of my mother, Anna Delia Conner, seriously declined. That next month, I returned back home to Fayetteville, North Carolina. I set up my desktop computer at my home in Fayetteville and showed my mother some of the music I had been working on while I was in school.

In the spring of 2006, I was back on campus at Fayetteville State University. The band at FSU was under the direction of the newly appointed director of bands, Mr. Timothy Chambers. I'm a firm believer that God puts us in places, situations and opportunities for a bigger purpose, even when we physically can't see them. As I made my way into the Rosenthal Performing & Fine Arts Building at FSU, I was immediately greeted by Mr. Chambers with a hug and fraternal grip. He welcomed me into his office.

During the spring semester, I was a full-time student, working two jobs and spending time with my parents after class. I was no longer a part of the marching band or pep band. But I kept my chops up in the concert band. But something was missing. So, with my mother's blessing, I joined the FSU pep band. That next season, I was back with the "Marching Bronco Express" playing the sousaphone. This season was, without a doubt, my very *last* season as a college band member. I just knew it. The band was much smaller than the bands I participated in at A&T. But man, the sounds that came out of that band room were simply amazing! The pen, creativity and pedagogy of Mr. Chambers is something I still strive to achieve today as a high school band director.

I defiantly had my moments of struggle because I was used to doing things a certain way for so long. However, I was quickly reminded where I was and that a good leader learns how to adapt to their surroundings. The season was one of the most amazing and fulfilling band seasons I'd had in years. When I used to arrive home after practices and games, I shared my excitement and the things I'd learned with my mother. She and Mrs. Chambers developed a relationship at the local dialysis center throughout that year, which made the bond between my family and Mr. & Mrs. Chambers remarkably close. Unfortunately, later that year on the day of my last performance at FSU, my mother was called home on November 4, 2006. My main supporter was no longer here to motivate me or listen to my stories. Most importantly, she wouldn't see my walk across the stage for graduation. My college band career was officially over.

In the spring of 2007, with the help, prayers and encouragement from family and friends from A&T and FSU, I jumped back into my undergraduate studies full steam ahead. I was more focused than ever, and I had one of my best semesters academically. School, work, individual practice, required rehearsals and home. That was the name of game. Later that semester, I was approached by two of the drum majors from that previous season. We had a conversation about the band and how great the potential of next season could be. I shared with them that I was officially old and didn't have the desire to march another season. They shared with me how they felt and suggested I'd be a great addition to the drum major squad. In all honesty, I knew my body was in no shape to march another season, let alone be up front as one of the leaders of the band.

I attended church one Sunday and heard a sermon about God's plans being bigger than ours. This message resonated with me that Sunday. I decided to get in shape for one last season. The audition process was intense. But mentally, I was prepared. All of my struggles and training had led up to this moment. There were close to eight others who tried out, but there was only one slot available. After it was all said and done, my number was called and one of my lifetime goals was finally achieved. The two other drum majors and I began our training later in the spring, under the leadership of Mr. Timothy Chambers. We helped lead one of the greatest editions of the Marching Bronco Express in the history of Fayetteville State University during the fall of 2007.

In the spring of 2008, it was finally my time to complete my senior recital, walk the stage, and earn my degree from the university that started it all. As much as I would like to say that this was the last time, I suited up in a college band uniform later that year during my first year of serving as a high school band director. The FSU "Marching Bronco Express" was selected to participate in the annual Honda Battle of the Bands in Atlanta, which was my last official college HBCU band performance.

My HBCU band experience and journey, although very unorthodox, was literally second to none! I was able to experience two different band programs that provided a perspective that molded and shaped me as an educator, musician and mentor. I've been told that everything happens for a reason. I would not be the person I am today without my HBCU and, more importantly, my HBCU band experience. Love, family, loyalty, showmanship, pageantry, tradition and history are all characteristics of each HBCU band program. It is one that creates lifelong friends and bonds that will never be broken. As HBCU band alums, our experience is much different than the typical HBCU student. While others are ending their academic day, we are just beginning rehearsal. While others are partying on the weekend, we are traveling across the country or entertaining the home crowd.

Our nights are long, and our mornings are extremely early.

But one thing is for sure: We would not trade our HBCU band experience for the world.

About Charles M. Conner, M.M.Ed.

A native of Fayetteville, NC by way of Brooklyn, NY, Charles M. Conner graduated from Westover High School. He received his Bachelor of Arts in Music Degree from Fayetteville State University with additional undergraduate studies at North Carolina Agricultural & Technical State University, where he was under the baton of Dr. Harold Bray, Dr. Johnny B. Hodge, Dr. Kenneth G. Ruff, and Mr. Timothy Chambers. While at North Carolina A&T State University, Charles (Chuck) was a member of the World Renowned "Blue & Gold Marching Machine" playing the Trombone and Baritone. During his tenure at A&T, he served as a Section Leader, Student Conductor and Arranger, Trombonist in the University Concert, Symphonic, and Jazz Band. While at Fayetteville State University, he served as a Student Conductor & Arranger, and Drum Major for the "Marching Bronco Express". As a member of the University Concert Band at FSU, he played the French Horn, Trombone, and Tuba. While attending Fayetteville State, he studied the Trombone, Euphonium, and Tuba under Dr. Neal Finn.

Upon graduation, Charles began his profession career in 2008 as the Director of Bands at Hoke County High School located in Raeford, NC. During his seven-year tenure at Hoke County High School, several ensembles earned superior ratings and National Performance invitations within the Wind Ensemble, Concert Band, Jazz Band, and the "Mighty Marching Bucks" Marching Band. Outside of his duties within the performing arts, he also served as the freshman and junior varsity head boys basketball coach. In 2015, Charles moved to Chicago, IL to serve on the South Side of Chicago as the Founding Director of Bands at Butler College Preparatory Charter School. Within a four-year span, he was able to create, develop, and establish a full instrumental music curriculum, concert band, jazz band, drum line, and The "Incomparable Marching Lynx" from scratch. In 2017, Charles continued his advanced studies at the prestigious VanderCook College of Music in Chicago IL, where he received his Master of Music Education Degree and was selected as the graduate class president for his class in the summer of 2020. His graduate thesis is entitled "The History and Impact of HBCU Band Programs in America." During his time at VanderCook, he participated in the graduate Wind Symphony, Jazz Band, Concert Chior, and studied Jazz Improvisation (Trombone) and Applied Saxophone underneath the Director of Jazz Studies at VanderCook, Associate Professor Anthony G. Kidonakis. In 2019, he moved to Las Vegas, NV where he currently serves as the Director of Bands and Performing Arts Department Chair at Canyon Springs Law & Leadership Academy High School.

As a classical and jazz musician, Charles has performed with the F-S-O (Fayetteville Symphony Orchestra), The Chicago State Community Jazz & Concert Band, served as a guest conductor of the Hoke County All District Middle School Honor Band, and Fayetteville State University Concert Band. In addition to his performance experience, he has been provided the opportunity as a clinician, guest conductor, and music arranger for several high schools and colleges throughout the country.

Charles M. Conner is a member of Kappa Kappa Psi National Honorary Band Fraternity, Inc. and Alpha Phi Alpha Fraternity Inc. He currently resides in Henderson, NV with his fiancé' Dr. Lanecha Williams, daughter Evelyn, son Ahmir, and their dog Bella.

Ernest Stackhouse

Band Changed My Life

Ernest Stackhouse

South Carolina State University

It's funny how life works out sometimes. Here I am, a Fine Arts Program Administrator and 20+ year veteran band director … who quit band in the eighth grade. I remember the day I was put into band class as a seventh grader in the Beck Middle School Band, like it was yesterday. My mom didn't request it, and I didn't, particularly, care to be in that class. I was more of an artist. The band was under the direction of a silver-haired lady who ran the band like a Navy Seal Team. She was tough. We had about forty kids in my class, but we could hear a pin drop. Being in that environment wasn't at the top of my list. It wasn't how I wanted to start my middle school experience.

I lived in Westside Apartments, better known as "The Projects". At that time, kids from my neighborhood were not into extracurricular activities. They were barely into curricular activities at all. As a result, many of the guys from my neighborhood never made it to high school, let alone graduation. But here I was, sitting in band class, alongside students from mostly middle-class backgrounds, learning how to play an instrument. One day, the director asked all of us what instrument we were interested in learning. I was from a single-parent home. Even at that young age, I knew my mother couldn't afford to purchase an instrument. On that day, the kids were screaming with excitement. "Trombone! Saxophone! Trumpet!" I just sat there. When the director finally got to me, I shrugged.

"I don't know." I acted like I didn't understand the question or know what the instruments were, even though I understood perfectly. So, the director, probably sensing the real reason I refused to answer, just moved on to the next kid. After class, she asked me if I'd be interested in playing the tuba. It was actually a white sousaphone made of fiberglass that sat in the back of the instrument storage room. It was a school-owned instrument, so my mother wouldn't have to make monthly payments. I quickly agreed. As time went on, I practiced the sousaphone in the courtyard of our apartment building, drawing a lot of attention and ridicule. Most of the reactions from the neighborhood kids ranged from confusion to amusement. Many of them asked me, "Why do you have a toilet bowl around your neck?" as they practiced their hoop dreams by shooting wads of candy wrappers down the large bell of my instrument. I must admit. It had to have been a weird sight to see a kid walking home to the projects with a sousaphone. I'm lucky no one realized the thousands of dollars it was worth.

One day, the director asked Shawn, the other tuba player, to play a line in the book. Then, she asked me to do the same. After I attempted to play, she noted that my tone had not improved as well as Shawn's and made it clear that he was a better player. I was crushed. I didn't like being embarrassed in front of the entire class. So, at the start of my eighth-grade year, I quit band. Even though I was no longer in band, I had developed a love for instrumental music. So, in the ninth grade, I joined the band program at Georgetown High School. I had not played an instrument in over a year, but the weirdest thing happened when I started playing tuba again. I was *good*. I mean really good! I was one of the best tuba players at the school. Then, I auditioned for district and regional band. I always ranked high amongst all tuba players in my region.

Mr. Tyrone Singleton, a South Carolina State University alum, was the high school band director who really set me on my path. He molded me into an even better tuba player and lover of music in general. But more than that, he was the father figure and role model I needed at that very delicate moment of my life. He was the best thing that could have happened to me at that time.

I am from Georgetown, South Carolina, a small town that most describe as "in between Myrtle Beach and Charleston" on the beautiful coastline of The Palmetto State. This area of the state is referred to as "the lowcountry" because it's home to all the towns and cities that lay below the Sandhills (the ancient seacoast, which runs the width of the state). Georgetown has a thriving tourist industry due to its history as the epicenter of commerce during the rice plantation era of the slave trade. However, there are two Georgetowns. The one I just described, and another one where well-paying jobs are few and far in between and most minorities live in poverty. I, of course, am a proud product of the latter.

In the fall of 1993, I was an eleventh-grade band student at Georgetown High School. We were preparing to compete in a mid-October band competition in Orangeburg, South Carolina. Upon arriving at the competition, many of my bandmates were buzzing with excitement because, unlike me, they knew we were about to experience an exhibition performance by South Carolina State University's Marching 101 at the conclusion of the event. During these days, The Marching 101 was God-like in the state of South Carolina. I'd never seen a college band in person, though I had watched hours upon hours of video tapes. This, of course, was well before YouTube and Facebook.

We had just finished our performance at the competition as charter buses rolled up behind the stadium. All the high school band students in the audience instantly let out a huge cheer of excitement!

When The Marching 101 entered the field, I was simply amazed. Every note the band played was mesmerizing. The sound was like that of a well-tuned orchestra that had studied with jazz musicians. Every note the tubas played, I could feel them resonating up through the bleachers and into my chest. I had never heard tubas like that before. I was blown away! Then, they played the song that changed my life forever: "One Last Cry" by Brian McKnight. The entire audience was standing throughout their performance, much like a party scene. But during this particular song, people were swaying back and forth in complete silence. It was a magical moment, one of the few times I had goosebumps from a marching band arrangement. I was sold! I knew at that moment that I was going to South Carolina State University. I was going to be a band director, and I was going to strive to have a band that sounded like that one day.

When I got to school that following week, I quickly made my way to the band room to hound Mr. Singleton for more information about The Marching 101. Of course, he was happy to oblige, having marched on the band in the late seventies. Little did I know, he was a former drum major! Over the course of that year, he told me countless stories about the SCSU band and its legendary director, Mr. Ronald J. Sarjeant. When I became a senior, Mr. Singleton arranged an audition session with South Carolina State's band staff. I was awarded a large band scholarship! I knew I wanted to go to SCSU, but to have a free ride was unimaginable! For this, I am forever indebted to him. If it wasn't for this scholarship, I would have had no means to obtain the education I so desperately needed.

In 1995, I attended South Carolina State University and majored in Music Education. Attending SCSU was one of the greatest decisions I've ever made. Having the opportunity to learn from legendary professors like Ronald Sarjeant, Tim Hinton, Dr. Barbara Vaughn, and Lameriel Ridges was a life-changing experience. Performing with collegiate ensembles such as The Marching 101 and The SCSU Wind Ensemble were great experiences that I will never forget. To make it even sweeter, as a member of the band at South Carolina State, I met a beautiful violinist and French horn player from Greenville, South Carolina, who would later become my wife.

I don't know where I'd be if band was not a part of my life. Band, and music in general, is a distinct part of who I am. And to think, I almost gave it all up in the eighth grade.

Isn't it funny how life works out?

About Ernest Stackhouse

Ernest Stackhouse is a native of Georgetown, South Carolina and a proud graduate of South Carolina State University where he studied under Ronald Sarjeant and Dr. Barbara Vaughn. He then matriculated to The Graduate School at The University of North Carolina at Greensboro where he studied under Dr Patricia Sink and Dr David Teachout. He is a member of Kappa Kappa Psi National Honorary Band Fraternity, Phi Mu Alpha Sinfonia Professional Music Fraternity, and Kappa Alpha Psi Fraternity Inc.

Mr. Stackhouse has 20 years of teaching experience and has served as Fine Arts Program Administrator, Band Director, Teacher, and Mentor to thousands of students ranging from grades K – 12. He takes pride in being able to reach students at any level of learning; beginner, intermediate, and advanced. Mr. Stackhouse has directed ensembles ranging from 16-piece Jazz Ensembles, advanced Wind Ensembles, to 150-member Marching Bands all of which received multiple superior ratings at competitions and festivals in multiple states. He is most proud of his students who have earned scholarships to various colleges and universities across the country totaling over eighteen million dollars.

Mr. Stackhouse has worked as a well-respected Music Educator for Darlington County Public Schools in Darlington, South Carolina, Twiggs County Public Schools in Jeffersonville, Georgia, and Houston Independent School District in Houston, Texas. He has also been recognized by numerous school boards for achievement in his profession, including being recognized as Teacher of the Year three times throughout his career. His proven leadership skills, unique musical abilities, dedication to education, and passion for all forms of music has, most recently, earned him the position of Fine Arts Director for Twiggs County Public Schools.

In his spare time Mr. Stackhouse serves as the Editor-In-Chief for www.BlockUsUp.com, a website chronicling the historical achievements and current impact of HBCU bands and their legendary band directors. He also serves as President of The

Advocates for Music & Music Education Association (www.ammea.org), a non-profit organization founded in the state of South Carolina whose mission is to cultivate, support, and enhance Music and Music Education throughout the state.

He is happily married to his wife, Jennifer, of 17 years and they have been blessed with three beautiful children; EJ, Raegan, and Kaydence.

Chase Arrington

Perseverance, Accountability, Commitment, Dedication & Loyalty

Chase Arrington

North Carolina A&T State University

I am humbled by the opportunity to provide a view of my time at North Carolina Agriculture & Technical State University and the Blue & Gold Marching Machine (BGMM). I started following the BGMM during the mid-90s. Being from Halifax County, North Carolina, collegiate bands were something we rarely had the opportunity to see. Therefore, I appreciate the BGMM's very own Christy Walker, who created www.the5thQuarter.com. This provided my first view into black college marching bands. I was a mere eighth grader who desired to study any and all things band related. Finally, I felt like I had found "my people". In high school, I reached out to several individuals through the forum to express my interest in attending NC A&T State University and participating in the marching band. During my high school marching band days, we participated in several black college homecoming parades. Through these events, I was able to see and experience the black college homecoming game experience.

I entered the band in 2002 under the direction of the late great Dr. Johnny B. Hodge. We entered the band room for our first music rehearsal. Dr. Hodge carried the infamous five-inch binder out of his office, laid it on the podium, and my heart beat faster and faster. I asked myself, "What did I do? Am I really prepared for this?" He asked us to take out the Battle Hymn Chorale. I heard the band play this in person, but something about *this* time was different. As instruments came up and the band said, "Blow!" I may have stopped breathing for a few moments. As we got toward the middle of the song, and Dr. Hodge's conducting pattern got bigger, broader and more intense, I stopped and looked around. I noticed so many of my crab brothers and sisters do the same thing because we finally had arrived at our new home in the BGMM.

There are a few moments that I hold near and dear in memory. In 2002, we braved the trip to Florida A & M University to face The Marching 100. This was my first time seeing The Marching 100 in person. We performed post-game and what happened after the game is what I will highlight. We marched off the field after performing, then blocked up in front of The Hundred! It was time: the BGMM versus The Hundred! We exchanged several songs and received so much praise from spectators. This was the battle of the season, and I was part of it! Dr. Hodge was asked to leave the stadium by police. But Dr. White and other members of The Marching 100 started yelling, "Let them play! Let them play!" This is what the Black college experience is all about!

In the spring of 2004, I made the decision, with two of my fellow trumpet players, to join the Mighty Iota Zeta Chapter of Kappa Kappa Psi National Honorary Band Fraternity, Inc. I entered the process with an open mind, hoping to just make it out of what I knew to be a challenging, yet memorable experience. I recall a big brother asking, "Chase, do you know why we chose you?" He told me I was chosen to be part of this process because the chapter saw me as a section leader. So, when I became a brother of Kappa Kappa Psi, I waited my turn to be recognized by Dr. Ruff in the fall of 2004.

When I received a call from him midday in September, Dr. Ruff said, "You are now the trumpet section leader. Goodbye." He hung up. Only Dr. Ruff could do that and people not take offense to it. Once class was over, Dr. Ruff knew I was making my way to his office. We went to the plot and talked about the change in leadership in September. He said he didn't think I wanted to be the section leader since I'd never expressed interest. I thought to myself, *A closed mouth does not get fed.* Once I became section leader, I found my voice. That voice was provided through the support and process of the Blue and Gold Marching Machine and Kappa Kappa Psi.

The journey through the years in Kappa Kappa Psi, and leadership in the band program, afforded me the opportunity to identify my purpose in life: to teach. I learned how to take challenging situations and make meaningful impacts to create productive outcomes for future successes. If I could go back and do it all over again, I would make the same choices in joining the band program and Kappa Kappa Psi; however, my approach to things would be different. One thing that Kappa Kappa Psi taught me is to learn and accept different viewpoints that people have regarding their morals and values. Dr. Ruff told me, "Chase, you have to learn to finesse your attitude and approach." Dr. Ruff never denied my results, but he taught me that I could achieve the same results through compassion. Dr. Ruff taught me to trust the process and to learn how to coach people to do what you do, especially in your absence. Many people say that it's harder to teach other people what comes naturally to you. There is no such thing as something coming "naturally". You must practice in order to strengthen any skill. Do not dismiss the journey because you have arrived at the destination. That is something I continue to remind myself as I connect with current BGMM members. I learned that I had to begin coaching others, and believing in others to do the right thing, even when I was not around. Simply stated, I had to learn to trust!

I never imagined being a section leader in the BGMM. From 2004 to 2006, I had the most amazing years leading the trumpets into battle! Each year provided growth opportunities and ways to build a fellowship through culturally responsive leadership. I saw what each trumpet player needed or desired. Differentiation of instruction was part of the practice I utilized during sectionals and building camaraderie for meaningful lasting relationships for a lifetime. Some of my closest friends, brothers and sisters are *Scream Machine*! I would trade nothing for the love and support shown to me when I was their leader. To be trusted by your peers is an experience I will cherish forever.

In 2005, we received brand new uniforms. This was another exciting time for the BGMM. I remember the Thursday night game on ESPNU against Hampton University. Additionally, I gained a co-section leader: ReShonda Thompson. We played "mom and dad" roles within the section. I was the accountability leader, and she was the compassionate, understanding leader. She taught me how to listen to the section and, through those voices, find ways to increase each person's capacity within the organization. I was excited for the BGMM and the trumpets. The sound of the band gelled through the strength of Chief Arranger, Aaron Campbell. Gary Bryant provided a fresh approach to drills and field show designs. These were exciting because we started facing "home" more and more, and the sound remained consistent toward the press box.

In 2006, I had the opportunity to finally connect with Assistant Director of Bands for the BGMM, the late great Mr. Brian E. Millsapp. After seeing his bands at James B. Dudley High School, and the accolades they received, I knew we were destined for greatness! His teachings from the podium commanded respect and the best! One of his favorite quotes was, "Discipline is at the pinnacle of success!" Being one of the founders of the Scream Machine and having one of the absolute best trumpet sections in 1994, I was honored to sit in his ensembles. I was honored to receive compliments during my time as section leader and, in 2007 and 2008, as a staff member working with the high brass and woodwinds!

Upon graduation, I joined the alumni band to continue the legacy and tradition of loyalty with the BGMM. The Greatest Homecoming on Earth (GHOE) is my favorite time of the year. It is a holiday for the community of Greensboro and surrounding areas! I can see my friends, connect with frat brothers, and remember the love of being an Aggie!

These experiences at North Carolina Agriculture & Technical State University molded me into the individual I am today. As an educator, I can take the tools the BGMM taught me and apply it to my career: *perseverance, accountability, commitment, dedication and loyalty*. As I conclude, a quote by Shannon L. Alder resonates with me: "Carve your name on hearts, not tombstones. A legacy is etched into the minds of others and the stories they share about you."

This quote reaches me in multiple ways. North Carolina Agriculture & Technical State University and the BGMM carved its name in my heart forever.

About Chase Arrington

Chase Arrington is a school administrator with Guilford County Schools in Greensboro, NC. Chase is a native of Halifax County, NC where he grew up in Enfield, NC and attended Halifax County Public Schools. His parents, Leon and Retha Arrington are his biggest supporters and provided strong foundation for his education and career choices.

Chase attended North Carolina A&T State University located in Greensboro, NC and earned a Bachelor of Science in Mathematics. He never saw himself in education, however God continued pulling on his heart and found himself falling in love with teaching, mentoring and supporting communities much like his own throughout the state of North Carolina. One of his motivations while in Guilford County Schools as a middle school mathematics teacher for nine years was to provide the necessary support to students of color from grades 6 – 8 in accelerated math courses. He saw there was a need to provide an extra layer of sustenance as students of color faced challenges maintaining the necessary requirements to remain in accelerated math courses throughout grades 6 - 8. His belief is that any student can access curriculum, however each student will access it at various entry points which makes learning and teaching exciting for an educator. His goal as a classroom teacher was not to have every student fall in love with math as he did but to allow them to know how to problem solve beyond the world of math and the school building.

Chase became a leader within his school building, so he took the leap of faith and earned a Master of School Administration from the University of North Carolina at Greensboro. As he continued to find ways to support not only students, but he also continued to collaborate with community stakeholders to provide the best possible equitable education to all students he encountered. In his role as a school administrator, he is an instructional leader by coaching teachers to support students culturally and academically.

Chase is in his third year as assistant principal at Western Guilford Middle School. Previously, Chase was Assistant Principal in 2016 -2018 at Forsyth Academy Charter School in Winston-Salem, NC and taught mathematics from 2007-2016 at Mendenhall Middle School, where he was selected Teacher of the Year in 2011. He obtained his Master of Education in Education Policy and Leadership from The American University, his Master of School Administration from the University of North Carolina at Greensboro, and his Bachelor of Science in Professional Mathematics from North Carolina A&T State University. Chase currently participates in the Guilford Aspiring Leaders Academy for the 2020 -2021 school year to focus on men of color in assistant principal roles to prepare them for principalships in the future. Chase also participated in the 2019 – 2020 New Leaders Assistant Principal Leadership Academy as well as the 2017 – 2019 William C. Friday Fellowship for Human Relationships through the Wildacres Leadership Initiative. As a leader, Chase focuses on a commitment to ensuring high scholastic achievement for all students through an equity-focused lens to hold himself and staff accountable for outcomes.

He participates with his fraternities within the community to support cultural arts through music as a Spring 2004 initiated of the Iota Zeta Chapter of Kappa Kappa Psi National Honorary Band Fraternity, a Spring 2017 initiate of the Iota Epsilon Chapter of Phi Mu Alpha Sinfonia of America, and academic achievement and leadership opportunities as a Spring 2009 initiate of the Kappa Lambda Chapter of Alpha Phi Alpha Fraternity. Phi Mu Alpha affords him the opportunity to participate in the Mills Music Mission where he gathers with fraternity members to provide musical selections to nearby hospitals, assistant living facilities, and retirement homes. Kappa Kappa Psi allows him the opportunity to continue mentoring students in the Blue & Gold Marching Machine on the campus of North Carolina A & T State University and Alpha Phi Alpha provides him the platform and vessel to give back through their national programs: Go-to-High-School, Go-to-College; A Voteless People is a Hopeless People; Project Alpha and Brother's Keeper.

In 2015, Chase was afforded the opportunity to participate in a three-week Park City Math Institute through The Institute for Advanced Study in Park City, Utah where he collaborated with math educators across the country to strengthen educational practices, curriculum, and approaches to problem solving.

During his college years, Chase participated in the University's Band Programs: The Blue & Gold Marching Machine, Wind Ensemble, and Pep Band playing trumpet and the piano for the wind ensemble. Additionally, he participated in the Mathematics Association of American and was inducted into Pi Mu Epsilon National Honorary Mathematics Society.

By participating in these organizations, he is part of three amazing organizations which are catalyst for our communities to raise awareness for students attending college, keeping the arts in the school, and most importantly bringing awareness to student voice within the community.

Chase is currently pursuing his Doctor of Education in Educational Leadership from the University of North Carolina at Greensboro. In his free time, Chase enjoys traveling with his family and friends, cooking, and playing with his Yorkshire Terrier, Kirby.

Herbert L. Seward III

Connection, Culture & Fellowship:
My HBCU Marching Band Experience

Herbert L. Seward III

Alabama State University

Honestly, my exposure to HBCU marching bands didn't start as early as some of my brothers and sisters who have generational family ties to the culture. My extended family is from Lawrenceville, Virginia, formerly home to one of the older HBCU institutions on the eastern seaboard, Saint Paul's College. Two of my aunts graduated from there. But I hadn't been exposed to marching bands in general, much less the rich, vibrant culture surrounding the craft. That all changed for me as a kid growing up in the D.C./Metro area during the mid- to late 1980s. Two catalysts started me on my journey into HBCUs and marching bands: the 'golden days' of Black Entertainment Television (BET), and Washington D.C.'s own vibrant marching band scene.

During those days, BET was a completely different media entity than it is now. My first intimate exposure to the culture came during those Saturday afternoons when the network showcased HBCU football in all its glory. It didn't matter who was playing. I couldn't help but be drawn to it. The more I watched, the more I was attracted. The bands particularly drew my attention because they were completely different than the things I was exposed to in school. Of course, as I got older, and got into high school, I got a chance to see the culture more. I had seen high school bands during the annual Georgia Avenue day parades that went down in northwest D.C. But the bands that got my attention were Howard University's "Showtime" Marching Band and the Marching Firebirds of the University of the District of Columbia. UDC, for some reason, always got my attention. The drum majors were awesome, and the band sounded twice their size going down the parade route to Howard's campus. In hindsight, it's pretty ironic that I was drawn to watching the Firebirds and Showtime because both programs had a huge influence on my journey into the HBCU marching band world.

Fast forward to my junior year at Eleanor Roosevelt High School, of course, I was knee-deep into the things most high school juniors are during that period. My buddy Wesley Hoover and I would sit in Mrs. Wagner's ensemble class and shoot the breeze about everything under the sun. But mostly, we talked about where we were going to school after high school. It was during one of those conversations that Wes invited me to meet up with him and his father over at UDC for a 'jam session' of sorts. It was UDC, so I was excited about the experience. Wesley's dad was Mr. Lloyd Hoover. I knew that he was a music instructor of some kind. What I didn't know was that he was the band director of UDC's Marching Firebirds band program. That jam session was me, as a PG county high schooler, sitting in with some of the best college bandsmen in D.C. There were kids in there who were from all of the D.C. high school programs that I'd seen and heard about. And I was there with them, playing the same repertoire. Mr. Hoover ended up being my first collegiate band director, and Wesley became a lifelong friend.

When my senior year came and went, I decided to stay local and go to UDC. Those same upperclassmen who gave me the side-eye during that jam session welcomed me with open arms into the program, along with Mr. Hoover. It just felt right. From the hard practices to hanging out at Roy Rogers (a burger spot beside campus) afterward, I just knew that campus was going to be home. Unfortunately, UDC's plans for the future didn't include the band program. It was one of the first departments the school had to cut because of funding reductions from the city. The scholarships that came with the program went as well. Needless to say, I was disappointed. The connections I made there were real. UDC marching band members ended up transferring to other schools. Many ended up across town at Howard University. I wasn't sold on staying home for school. So, the incident with UDC's program was kind of a pretext for me to act on my urge to go away to school.

After talking a lot with my parents, in 1993, I decided to go away to school. Alabama State wasn't initially on my transfer radar list. I was looking to stay closer to home, specifically North Carolina A&T or Norfolk State. But the low cost of out-of-state tuition for the school drew me to check it out. I stepped on campus and immediately fell in love with the place. I also decided that I wanted to still march. I found out later that Mr. Hoover had a great deal to do with me getting consideration for Bama State's program before getting on campus for an audition. Dr. Danny Davis, who was the band director for the Mighty Marching Hornets at the time, contacted me a good two months or so before I made the trek to Montgomery. He instructed me to record an audition tape for him to evaluate. I got on campus, expecting to have a second audition. I ended up immediately donning the telltale combat boots, black basketball shorts, and Gold "Question Mark" t-shirts that newcomers to the Alabama State University band program had to wear their first season. I experienced many emotions during that first week of pre-drill, but I mainly experienced relief and happiness. I'd found the same kind of connection that I had when I was back home in D.C. The culture was different, and my peers were from tons of different places across the country. However, the camaraderie was the same. I'd found a second home. My experiences at both UDC and Alabama State pushed me to grow in ways that I couldn't have if I had decided on going to a non-HBCU. It fostered friendships and connections that will be with me for a lifetime. Those connections have been a beacon for me in *every* aspect of my life.

When school ended, I served in the Navy in further pursuit of a career in Information Technology. That enlistment and service took me to over twenty-five countries. At the time, those places seemed far away from the connections I'd built during in school. Turns out, those connections weren't as far away as I thought. I was stationed in Norfolk, Virginia, which put me close to both Norfolk State University and Hampton University. Needless to say, I spent a good bit of my spare time traveling to games and checking out bands. I also found more like-minded friends who had their own respective connections to the culture and craft. I have a lifetime of *great* memories over the years that involve HBCU bands, music and the culture that binds those things together. For me, there isn't a day that goes by where that connection isn't as strong as that first time walking into UDC's band room as a high school student or making it to the end of my first season at Alabama State and becoming a Marching Hornet. Two families. Two connections. The same bond.

Today, I've been an Information Technology professional for more than twenty years. I'm also a writer, covering HBCU athletics and culture. The roots for those skills were born out of those connections to the culture I made long ago. These days, I spend my time with the pen, sharing my experiences and love for HBCU marching band culture with young people who are discovering the joy that connection brings for the first time. My experiences are their experiences. I'm proud to be a link in the chain of that collective history of connection, love and fellowship for the craft. I hope reading about my journey inspires others to take that same leap into that fellowship.

The lifetime rewards to be had from those connections are priceless.

> *"The price of glory is high…"*
> – Mighty Marching Hornet Motto

About Herbert L. Seward III

Herbert L. Seward III is a product of Alabama State University and an alum of the school's storied 'Mighty Marching Hornets' marching band program. Mr. Seward is a United States Navy veteran and a 25-plus year Information Technology generalist and Cloud Computing Subject Matter Expert.

Herbert is also the host of a Technology Podcast aptly named 'The Black Techies' (http://www.theblacktechies.com) and a prolific writer and blogger.

Herbert also serves as a College Basketball Contributor for FanSided's 'Busting Brackets' online sports media platform (https://bustingbrackets.com/author/hsewardiii/), covering HBCU Division I basketball. Hallowed Hoops Ground (http://www.hallowedhoopsground.com) and View From The Sidelines (http://www.halftimeglory.com) are two blogs that Mr. Seward maintains that cover HBCU Marching Band Culture, and the basketball scene in the DC/Metropolitan area respectively.

Herbert's full writer portfolio can be found here at https://clearvoice.com/cv/HerbertSewardIII.

Herbert is a native of Washington, D.C. a proud parent, and a lover of all things BBQ, Tech, and HBCU Band/Culture related.

Jamie R. Brunson

The 101 Connection is Here…
Shake Your Pluuuume!
South Carolina State University Marching 101

Jamie R. Brunson

South Carolina State University

"R-U-B-B-E-R F-A-N-S… the Rubber Fans…and the 101…we love, we love, we love, we love you Marching 101, your funk is the best! Take your funk and give it to mine, to funk with the rest. If you like our funky sound, shake your rump, and get on down, 'cause we love you 101, the baddest band!"

On any given Saturday, you could hear the percussive sound of boots to bleacher stairs as The Marching 101 entered the stands from the pregame show. Plumes shaking, instruments flashing, and every voice chanting, expressing love for the incomparable Marching 101 of South Carolina State University. Football in Orangeburg, South Carolina is a huge deal. Whether it be recreation league, middle school, high school, or the tenacious Bulldogs of South Carolina State, the natives love football. Along with that love for football is a grand admiration for the artistry of halftime: the marching bands. The classic unwritten rule in Oliver C. Dawson Bulldog Stadium on the campus of South Carolina State University is, "No one leaves their seat until the halftime show is complete!" It was that kind of love that made being a member of The Marching 101 of South Carolina State University one of life's greatest experiences.

The Marching Band that we all know as The Marching 101 can trace its beginnings back to the year 1918 on the campus of The Colored Normal Industrial Agricultural and Mechanical College of South Carolina. The ensemble was described as a small regimental band. The band actually shared uniforms with the ROTC program at the school, as they provided the music for Sunday School, and wherever else they were needed. As transitions in directors occurred, and differences in their respective visions were carried out, the band evolved from being just a service band to becoming an integral part of the music department of the college. In 1964, the members and staff of the marching band decided to go with the nickname "Marching 101". The legacy, the history, and the great accomplishments of the South Carolina State Marching 101 continued as the band has had the opportunity to participate in major bowl parades, three Honda Battle of the Bands performances, and just recently, the inauguration of our 46th President of the United States, Joseph Biden. The Marching 101 band has set its mark amongst the giants in the HBCU band world.

Freshman year was the year of new beginnings. It was my first year being on a college campus, experiencing the unknown, meeting new people from different backgrounds, and most importantly, becoming a member of the world-renowned Marching 101. As a freshman in an HBCU band, I experienced a lot of different changes. In the HBCU band world, freshmen band members are given names of "endearment." One of those most commonly used nicknames is "crab". As a crab, it was our responsibility to be the best bandsman every day. Freshman year taught the new members a lot about discipline. You learned how to be on time, and most importantly, you learned great lessons about respecting protocol. Probably the most important lesson learned was how to master time management.

As with many organizations, The Marching 101 has many traditions. One of these traditions is something we call "crossing the tracks." Near the end of the parade route in Orangeburg, South Carolina, near the entrance of South Carolina State University, are a set of railroad tracks. Everyone has to "cross the tracks" to make it back onto campus. Once you successfully complete your first marching season, which culminates with the Orangeburg Christmas Parade, you are a full-fledged member of the Marching 101. As small of a detail as it may seem, it is a *big deal* to cross the tracks as a freshman in The Marching 101 Band. That call and response of,

"1-0....1!" has a new meaning when the band makes that left flank to head back toward the entrance of the campus. That was a huge part of the *pride* that was instilled from day one. My crab brothers and sisters who I met in the fall of 1996 became lifelong friends, many of whom I still talk to today. We can go days, weeks, months or even years without speaking. But once we see each other again, we pick up right where we left off.

Being in an HBCU band can be likened to being in a huge family. Yes, we fuss and fight. But at the end of the day, we're still willing to go to *war* for our brothers and sisters. One of the greatest attributes about being in any marching band is its inclusive nature. You could be a viable contributor and not even need to play an instrument. There are other especially important performance areas that give the "flare" to our HBCU bands. There is the color guard or flag line, the dance line, and the ever so important band managers. Everyone plays an integral part in the family structure. Specifically, in The Marching 101, it is the Tweety Byrds (Piccolos); Super Sonic Squeaks (Clarinets); Jazzy Brothers (Saxophones); Mellow Psi (Mellophones); Screaming Eagles (Trumpets); Ego Trippers (Baritones); Amtrak Express (Trombones); Thunder Brothers Incorporated (Tubas); Bongo Brothers Incorporated (Percussion); Electric Silk (Flag Line); Champagne (Dance Line); and the Kaped Krusaders (Drum Majors). Although we had our separate sections, we were all a big family. The friendships that were developed within these sections of The Marching 101 are some of the closest knit one could imagine. These relationships that were developed over time truly became one *huge* support system. This family is committed to checking on each other and helping each other, if any need arises.

One of the greatest takeaways is the organization's leadership development. Being a young leader in an HBCU band is not an easy task. My leadership journey began when I became section leader during my freshman year in the pep band. I was a leader in the band for the remainder of my time at South Carolina State University, even when I tried to escape it! Being a leader in the band taught me how to receive constructive criticism. I didn't always want to hear what was coming my way. But as I matured as a leader, I learned to remove personal feelings and focus on the issues at hand. Being a leader in the band also taught me to be an effective communicator.

As a leader, I received pertinent information from the band staff. It was my responsibility to relay the message to the multitude of personalities I was charged to lead.

One of the lasting impressions our band directors instilled in us was that, if we could be successful in leading a group of our peers, we could be successful in any realm of leadership. We quickly learned to understand and appreciate the leadership hierarchy in the band. This hierarchy extended from the director to the drum majors, to the section leaders, on down to the newest members of the band. Understanding this leadership hierarchy helped many of us thrive and excel in our respective careers.

Professionally, I am a middle school principal in South Carolina. Leaders from across our state attend a leadership institute every summer, which is held in Myrtle Beach. In my first year of attendance at this conference, it was a thrilling experience to witness the number of Marching 101 alumni who were serving their school districts in various leadership roles. It is that commitment to excellence in leadership that made all of my leadership experiences in The Marching 101 that much more worthwhile.

The life lessons, the leadership development, the road trips, and most importantly, the creation of lifelong friendships, are several of the reasons that make being a member of The Marching 101 such a great accomplishment. Whether it was our fierce rivalry with MEAC foes, such as Florida A&M University's "Marching 100" or North Carolina A&T's "Blue and Gold Marching Machine," or having the opportunity to face "The Human Jukebox" of Southern University or "The Aristocrat of Bands" of Tennessee State University in an HBCU classic, being a member of The Marching 101 opened up many doors. It gave us access to some of life's greatest opportunities and some lifelong friendships, which, I would not trade for anything. The HBCU band experience is *priceless*!

"Hail! Hail, dear alma mater! Hail! Hail, dear SCC! We'll defend and honor, love and cherish thee!"

About Jamie R. Brunson

Jamie R. Brunson is a 19-year veteran in education, and he currently serves as Proud Principal of Fairfield Middle School. Jamie has served as Assistant Principal of Instruction at Fairfield Central High School, Winnsboro, SC, Director of Guidance and Assistant Head Football Coach at Lower Richland High School, Hopkins, SC, where he was named the 2010-2011 Teacher of the Year. The Cameron, SC native is an alumnus of South Carolina State University, where he obtained a B.S. in Mathematics Education, an M.Ed. in Counselor Education, an Ed. S. in Educational Administration, and is currently a candidate for a Doctor of Education degree. While at SC State, Jamie was a member of the World Renowned Marching 101 Band, where he played tuba and sousaphone, and held the position of section leader for multiple years, and sat as principal tuba in the SC State University Wind Ensemble.

Brunson continues his love for music, by freelancing as an event DJ. Jamie first spun his way on the Disc Jockey scene in 2015. He has always been one to express himself through music. As he has continued to develop his craft as a disc jockey, he has established a reputation as one of the most innovative DJs of this generation. Through Rap, Hip-Hop, R&B, Jazz, NeoSoul, Oldies, Pop, Soul, Funk, Gospel, Top 40, and other genres, SC DJ Worm 803 is widely regarded as the "Administrator of the Turntables." As a skilled DJ, who does it "for the culture", he is one of the most sought-after disc jockeys in the Southeastern region.

Jamie has a passion for mentoring the youth, especially African-American males. He has a desire to help to guide young men into becoming good men who are productive contributors in society. He is a member of the South Carolina Association of School Administrators, South Carolina Alliance of Black School Educators, South Carolina Education Association, Phi Mu Alpha

SINFONIA, Tau Beta Sigma (Honorary), Life Member of Omega Psi Phi Fraternity, Inc., where he currently serves as Basileus (president) of the Epsilon Omega Chapter of Orangeburg, SC, Prince Hall Free & Accepted Masons, Ancient Egyptian Arabic Order Noble Mystic Shrine, and The 100 Black Men of Greater Columbia. He is married to the former Teesa Johnson of Bamberg, SC, and they have one daughter, Kennedy. They are members of Mount Carmel Baptist Church, Cameron, SC, where Jamie serves as a Deacon, Assistant Treasurer, and Director of all choirs.

David Matthews

The Defining Moment
David Matthews
Tennessee State University

During the summer of 2005, I received a letter from the Tennessee State University Aristocrat of Bands, informing me that I had been selected to serve as a clarinet section leader. I had never served as a section leader before. As a matter of fact, I'd never held any kind of major leadership position. Needless to say, I was a little apprehensive, yet encouraged, that my band directors saw leadership potential in me. It wasn't always that way, but I attribute much of that growth to my experience in the Aristocrat of Bands.

I've always been an introvert. If you were to ask people who knew me throughout my childhood, they'd likely say that I was really shy and quiet. I was regularly bullied in elementary and middle school, which led to poor self-esteem. I also tended to avoid negative situations and the spotlight as much as possible (partially because of negative feelings associated with bullying). Imagine how I felt entering band camp as a freshman in 2003, in a totally new environment, at a totally different school, in a totally different state.

Being a freshman in a collegiate marching band can be daunting. While you may have been one of the best musicians in high school, you're now surrounded by upperclassmen who are legitimate prodigies on their instrument. The Aristocrats' marching and playing style was vastly different than what I was used to in high school. However, one thing I really appreciated was TSU's insistence on looking and sounding good. It was this insistence that spurred me to develop the confidence I needed to succeed.

My first marching season was difficult, to say the least. Not only did I have to memorize a literal book of music, but I had to deal with learning a different style and endure teasing from some of the upperclassmen. Fortunately, I had gracious section leaders who kept me away from most of the troublemakers. Because TSU's marching style was different, I practiced hard to ensure my leg looked like a "chair" instead of tucked in. The muscle memory I'd formed after four years of high school had to be unlearned. I constantly practiced my music because our band directors frequently went down the line to see who knew their music. I also wanted to make sure that I stood out among the rest. I tend to have a bit of a competitive streak. I wanted to demonstrate that I could not only play just as well as the upperclassmen, but even better. Having a sharp marching style and competent playing ability helped me gain much more confidence. However, that would not have happened if TSU's band's ethos wasn't so centered around looking and playing well.

It was an unspoken rule that freshmen were "forbidden" to utter the word "Aristocrat" until after halftime at our homecoming game. We couldn't even wear the Aristocrat headband outside of performances. That might seem frivolous, but many of us saw it as something to aspire to. The word "aristocrat" evokes a level of sophistication and class that others do not have. You earn that privilege by completing the rigors of the marching band season and playing your instrument well. Indeed, there were some freshmen who dropped out and did not earn that title. However, by God's grace, I made it to the end. When we played the song "TSU Funk" during the fourth quarter at our homecoming game, I made sure to yell, "Aristocrat of Bands!" as loudly as I possibly could. I had earned the title of "Aristocrat," as well as the respect of the upperclassmen.

Another thing that led to a rise in my confidence was the sheer majesty of performing at a Historically Black College and University (HBCU) football game. In high school, I was used to performing in front of thousands of people. But now, I was performing for tens of thousands of people (millions if the game was televised). Hearing the Jackson State University Sonic Boom of the South, the South Carolina State University Marching 101, or the Florida A&M University Marching 100 across the stadium try to outmatch and outplay us was exhilarating.

Tennessee State University is the only HBCU in the Ohio Valley Conference. As such, we were only able to play a limited amount of football games against other HBCUs. That actually made us more competitive because we knew we needed to make the most of those three or four HBCU games. We'd often practice for hours, sometimes close to midnight, to ensure we performed at our best. At those games, we weren't freshmen and upperclassmen. We were The Aristocrat of Bands, and we came to battle.

Being in an HBCU band is more than just being a musical ensemble. It's about being a family. I'll never forget my grandparents calling me during the second semester of my freshman year, tearfully informing me that my mom had suddenly passed away. That semester was easily the hardest of my college career. My grades slipped drastically, and I had to figure out how to continue through college without my mom. However, the band rallied around to help me through that difficult period. It was in the band where I found people who cared about me and encouraged me.

My sophomore year was a little easier because I didn't have to worry about adjusting to a new school. If anything, this was my time to focus on improving my musical ability and to set an example as a newly minted upperclassman. At TSU, we often performed halftime drills in squads of four because it was easier and more precise to make the various formations that way. One person in each squad was designated squad leader to ensure the group executed the requisite maneuvers to create the formations to the beat of the music. I was fortunate to land a spot as a squad leader and enjoy my first taste of leadership.

In 2005, I was sitting at home, holding the letter asking me to be a clarinet section leader. I excelled at marching and playing, but now I had to somehow ensure that an entire musical section could do the same thing. I also knew that, as a junior, some of the seniors likely didn't see me as deserving of the position. On top of that, I'd be a man leading a section that predominantly consisted of women. I knew that my work was cut out for me. I knew respect needed to be earned.

Like my freshman year, my first band season as a section leader was difficult. I'm naturally soft-spoken. So, I had to learn how to project my voice and speak with authority. Any mistakes I made were amplified by the fact that I was in a leadership position. Fortunately, I had two other co-section leaders to help me adjust.

As a section leader, I was often put in uncomfortable situations. Some of the seniors tried to undermine my authority by embarrassing me in front of the section. Most of the time, I'd just grit my teeth and try to endure it. I hadn't yet developed the strength to stand my ground. I'd often look to the older, more experienced section leaders to see how they handled difficult people. However, one day the section was acting particularly unruly. I had everyone stand still at attention. I don't remember exactly what I said, but I was able to summon the courage to let the section know that I wasn't going to deal with their foolishness. Standing my ground, and being able to play well, went a long way in earning the respect of my peers.

In the grand scheme of my life, it may seem that being a section leader in a collegiate marching band is relatively insignificant. However, that experience reinforced my confidence in being a leader, despite my introverted personality. In 2006, I helped bring Alpha Nu Omega Fraternity, Inc. to the campus of TSU, and I became its chapter president. As a graduate assistant, I was able to teach programming courses to undergraduate students. Even in my current employment, I've been able to brief high-level senior officials in the U.S. government, as well as serve as a lead for multiple teams of highly skilled contractors.

Many people aspire to leadership. But it wasn't something I was initially interested in. However, I can definitely say that my experience in the Tennessee State University Aristocrat of Bands molded me into a more self-assured man, willing to lead in various aspects of my professional and personal life. The shy, quiet boy who entered band camp in 2003 became a confident, capable man who is willing to take on new challenges—all because of that defining moment at TSU.

About David Matthews

David Matthews, an Atlanta, GA native, currently lives in Northern Virginia with his beautiful wife and daughter. His educational background includes a B.S. in Computer Science from Tennessee State University and a M.S. in Computer Science from North Carolina A&T State University. After obtaining his Master's Degree, David worked several jobs at Freddie Mac and as a contractor at the Army National Guard before finally landing a career with the U.S. Government as a network engineer. David is currently certified as a Cisco Certified Network Professional and has amassed over a decade of experience in various computer technologies including networking, virtualization, digital forensics, and cyber security.

In 2017, David started The Black Techies Podcast, a platform dedicated to giving black people an outlet to talk about technology, gaming, and pop culture. Since its inception, The Black Techies Podcast has become one of the leading podcasts for black technologists and has interviewed both prominent and up and coming black YouTubers and content creators. The Black Techies have also been active in promoting competitive e-sports at Historically Black Colleges and Universities. An avid content creator himself, David started a YouTube channel called PacketStealer where he discusses gaming and technology news along with impressions of various video games.

Since 2017, David has been a freelance writer for TechSpot.com, an online tech news outlet with over 8 million monthly readers. He has written hundreds of stories concerning the latest in consumer tech news as well as featured stories about the iPhone X, Pixel 4 XL, and the rise and fall of Palm, Inc.

Derrick Black

A Casualty of Band Warfare

Derrick Black

North Carolina A&T State University

I remember it like it was five minutes ago. I saw the North Carolina Agricultural & Technical (A&T) State University marching band, also known as the "Blue & Gold Marching Machine" (BGMM), up close and personal for the first time on October 19, 1996. As part of the University Day morning activities, high school visitors from all around the state, and various parts of the nation, gathered inside the Corbett Sports Center gymnasium to be officially welcomed to the campus. Any current or former high school student knows that morning assemblies are often long and boring, regardless of the occasion. I do not remember the people who spoke first that morning, but I *do* remember every moment of entertainment when the BGMM marched inside. They had this swagger about them that resonated through every member, in every step, every musical note, and every dance routine move. I later found out that this is just the essence of what we call "Aggie Pride." But there were two specific reasons they were able to sell me into attending A&T so easily.

One reason was because they had just come home a week ago from a legendary battle against the "Marching 100" band of Florida Agricultural & Mechanical University (FAMU). The BGMM went to Tallahassee, Florida, put on a solid halftime show, and earned respect and a standing ovation from the crowd. Even though "The 100" was three times the size of the BGMM, A&T literally stood face-to-face with them in the fifth quarter (the band battle in the stands after the game). They went song for song, and earned their respect, as well.

The other reason was their band director. A band often takes on the attitude and the personality of its director. Dr. Johnny Baxter Hodge, Jr., affectionately known as "Doc", had no problem letting everyone know that this was his valley, and he would always be the baddest man in it. He was feisty, tenacious, relentless and aggressive—definitely someone you would rather have with you than against you. Therefore, his A&T bands had passion, hunger, energy and confidence. The BGMM knew they were the best, and they walked around wishing some "fishsammachee-at-best, rooty-poo band" *would* try to prove otherwise. Any of these other bands facing Doc and the BGMM got embarrassed in any stadium, on any given Saturday. A band like that, with that kind of leader, was one that I just *had* to join as soon as possible.

Band camp was an intense, but necessary period, which tested our physical, mental and musical endurance. My first game was the Aggie-Eagle Classic on August 30, 1997. Over 30,000 fans attended in Raleigh, North Carolina that day. I remember the excitement I felt at the chance to perform for all of them. We went on to entertain crowds in Washington, D.C.; Daytona Beach; Norfolk, Virginia; and Indianapolis, to name a few. Even the fans of the National Football League were treated to special BGMM halftime performances at Carolina Panthers games. We were continuing the high standard set by that 1996 band and all A&T bands before it. However, we still had unfinished business with the Marching 100.

The two bands had not been able to renew their rivalry since 1996.But all that changed in 1999. Both A&T and FAMU had football teams that were undefeated in the Mid-Eastern Athletic Conference (MEAC). A showdown on November 13, 1999 between FAMU and A&T would decide the conference championship. The entire season was on the line. So, we were not surprised to hear rumors that the Marching 100 would be making the trip to Greensboro, North Carolina to support their team. The Internet was buzzing about this potential rematch, especially on the 5th Quarter website, a forum where Black college band-a-holics talked smack, posted band clips, and debated on all things band-related. Most fans already understood that there would be a war taking place that day. At some point, the football teams would get to play their game, too. There could only be one winner that day. The Dr. Hodge in me reasoned that the game was in our house and this was our year. So, we *definitely* would not be losing that day.

Practices were intense, as every part of our performance that day had to be exactly right. I was so excited that I only slept for one hour the night before the game. One of my 5th Quarter friends, "Baloo" from Morgan State University, messaged me at 5a.m. on game day and asked if I was ready. Yes, I was ready. But I was not fully rested. I was a college student, though. So, I figured I could just power through the day anyway. I could rest after the war was over.

I made sure that I ate a good breakfast that morning. *Public service announcement:* Always eat breakfast on game day so you don't pass out on the field or in the stands from dehydration or lack of nutrients. This is especially important! We had to meet at the band room at 9:30 that morning. I finished eating and walked toward my friend's car to get my trombone out of the trunk. That was the last thing I remembered.

My lack of sleep caused me to immediately lose consciousness and have an epileptic seizure outside of the band hall. *Public service announcement two:* Get some sleep, too! I later found out that so many of my bandmates witnessed it and were scared for me. I wasn't able to participate in the band battle. I spent the rest of that morning, and part of the afternoon, in the hospital. I heard afterward that Doc told the band that the halftime show they would perform that day was dedicated to me. It meant the world to me to hear that later.

I woke up a few hours later in the hospital bed, accompanied by my parents, who had come from almost two hours away when they heard the news. I felt a lot more refreshed after the long nap. But when I heard the story of what happened, I immediately wondered about the game, and of course, the *war*. As the final medical test results came back, I was cleared to be discharged. I begged my dad to take me to the battlefield, Aggie Stadium. I was still weak, but he took me anyway. I made it just in time to see the final seconds of the fourth quarter count down. Our team had handled their business. A&T, 30. FAMU, 15. Just like that, we were

MEAC champions, and we would also go on to finish the season undefeated in the conference.

Moments after the game ended, I finally made my way up that stadium ramp and made eye contact with Doc. I still remember that tight hug he gave me like it was *one* minute ago. My bandmates cheered with delight. I could not stay for long because I needed to get more rest, but I stayed to watch the bands play a couple of songs at the beginning of their fifth quarter battle. They continued to battle nonstop for two and a half or three hours straight after the end of the game that day.

November 13, 1999 was a great day for many reasons. The MEAC football championship had been clinched. A band rivalry had been revived. Respect was earned on both sides of the field, and I received love and support from Doc and bandmates that I will never forget. I was excited to join the BGMM after that October day back in 1996.But I never could have anticipated the profound effect it would have on my life afterward. I learned about the values of hard work, dedication to excellence, and *loyalty,* which I hold dear to this day. There are no shortcuts to success. So, always be the hardest and smartest worker in the room. Commit to being the best, and never compromise that commitment. Last, but certainly not least, if you make sure to support your team members, especially when they are down, I promise they will remember it forever. If I could inspire one person as much as Doc and the band inspired me, then to God be the glory.

Rest in peace to the late, beyond great Director of Bands Emeritus of North Carolina A&T State University, Dr. Johnny B. Hodge, Jr., who passed away on May 5, 2013. I humbly dedicate this chapter to you, just as you dedicated your time, energy, spirit and life to so many of us.

About Derrick Black

Derrick Black is a former member of the North Carolina Agricultural & Technical State University "Blue & Gold Marching Machine", where he joined the ranks of the "Freight Train" trombone section in 1997. Derrick was born and raised in Oxford, North Carolina, and he now resides in Winston-Salem, North Carolina. When he is not reliving his marching band glory days around the house and with the Blue & Gold Marching Machine Alumni Band at homecoming, he spends most of his time loving on his wife and four children, working as a quality engineer in the healthcare technology industry, and tutoring in higher-level mathematics courses. You can connect with Derrick on Facebook at facebook.com/derrick.black.568 or on Twitter @DerrickBlack9.

Chevis Anderson

Still Approaching: My Life & Times at Delaware State University

Chevis Anderson

Delaware State University

Three days before my eighteenth birthday, I was at band camp. I was hot and sweating in the August heat, outside in shorts and a tee-shirt, standing at attention.

"I bet not see anyone move!" yelled the drum major.

I stood there, afraid to move. Out of nowhere, a bee stung me on my knee. I yelled out "Shit!"

His response is, "Whoever said that, give me two laps." My squad leader, Orlando, yelled out, "Sir, he got stung, *but* he didn't move."

The drum major blew the whistle, "Everyone at ease." I fell in pain as he came over and said, "Welcome to band camp." From that point on, I knew I was going to be a part of something wild and crazy.

I developed a love for music when, at the age of six, I picked up my father Roland's trumpet. I was able to produce a sound. From that moment on, my mother, Elaine, encouraged me in everything related to music. As a graduate of the Philadelphia Public School System, I attended Darroff Elementary School, which had a music class, but very few instruments. However, that did not stop me. I wanted to learn, so I used what they had, which was the clarinet. I learned to play it and developed a love for woodwinds.

My sister LaDonda, who I admired, had just graduated from Overbrook High School in Philly and received a band scholarship to Cheney University. When I helped her move onto campus, seeing all those black students, and hearing the band welcome everybody on campus, was my first true experience with an HBCU and an HBCU band.

After attending Darroff, I went on to attend Sulzberger Middle School. My mother bought me my first alto saxophone, which she had gotten from her co-worker. It was the first of many instruments I would ultimately own. I followed in my big sister's footsteps and went to attend Overbrook High School. I joined the high school band and choir. Once again, the instruments at the school weren't in any acceptable working condition. In my senior year, I decided to save my money and buy a tenor saxophone, just like Charlie Parker. Upon graduating from Overbrook High, I was accepted to five institutions. But it was only one that had the best options and cost at the time. So, I chose Delaware State University.

So, the first day of camp, I was already known as the guy who got stung. There was nothing I could do about it but laugh. I was sitting in the band room, finishing my first music rehearsal. Our band captain Jen yelled out at the end of practice, "Stay off the fifth!"

Our drum major echoed her, "Yeah, stay off the fifth. If we catch you, it's laps!"

I looked over to my section leader and asked, "The fifth? What's the fifth?"

"I'll tell you in sectionals," he said.

Later that night, Tenorsax2damax, my 5th quarter screenname, was born and I've never looked back! The 5thquarter.com was the website for any and everything HBCU marching band related. This is what started my interest in band media. This site gave me my true voice and developed my passion for HBCU bands and culture. I was so involved with the 5th Quarter that I got to know the owners, Christy Walker and Mike Lee. Eventually, I became one of the 5th's first media correspondents, which allowed me access to the battle of bands (BOTB), exclusive interviews with prominent band directors, and behind-the-scenes footage of several HBCU bands. With my knowledge and experience in media, I developed my own company, MilRo Entertainment, LLC. A lot of great things happened my freshman year, but nothing more memorable than my first homecoming game.

It was homecoming 2000, DSU versus South Carolina State University. Mr. Johnson, our band director, showed up to the band room with a neck brace on. All of the freshmen were concerned. The upperclassmen said nothing at all.

He said, "I'll be okay by the time halftime starts. Let's warm up." So, we continued to warm up, tune and march to the stadium. We lined up for the opening fanfare "2001 Space Odyssey". He started conducting. Everything looked normal at first. As soon as it got to the climax of the fanfare, he snatched the neck brace off, threw it in the air, and continued to conduct from the 45 to the 45-yard line on the field. This man had the entire stadium on its feet as he ended the last note with a split and blew a kiss to the crowd. This got the band super hyped, and our school went on to win that game. This was my first homecoming, and it was amazing! After seeing my first step show, it wasn't long before I started asking questions about the band fraternity.

As I researched, I found out that, not only did DSU have a chapter established, but I found out who started it. It was during the tenure of band director, Mr. Brock, that he recommended chartering a chapter on DSU's campus in 1982. It later became known as the Eta Psi Chapter in 1983. The founders of the Eta Psi Chapter were Vincent Adkins, Clifford Cephas, Dorian Jerome Allen, Sidney Sessoms, Sekou Foure Reid-Bey and Paul Freeman. Two years later, seven young ladies, Kendell Lyons, Margaret Steele, Thelma Smith, Monique Upshur, Terri Ballard, Cynthia Suggs, and Regina Paige established the Eta Iota chapter of Tau Beta Sigma National Honorary Band Sorority.

A few fellas from the band and I reached out to the headquarters of Kappa Kappa Psi and Tau Beta Sigma to see what we had to do to bring the chapter back. After much discussion and letter writing, I'm proud to say that in the spring of 2003, eight men by the names of: Chevis Anderson, Stradivari Baynard, Eumir Brown, Ricky English (deceased), Orlando Glasby, Jahi Robinson, James Smith, and Al Weal re-chartered the Eta Psi Chapter. Al

Davis, Tory Smart and Lonnie Elias were made honorary members. Also, Tau Beta Sigma was re-chartered in the fall of 2003 by six young ladies: Kadian Cephas, Ticoya Mullen, Tamara Reaves, Recheinda Scott, Yvonne Lomax, and Ayeola Coleman, and two honorary members, Jennifer Thompson and Tory F. Smart.

Homecoming 2003, DSU versus Morgan State University, will be a day that will forever be in my brain as the day of fun and chaos. I was elected Chapter President of the Eta Psi and Educational Dean of the current line at that time, later Named "Six Degrees of Sui-ψ-de", James Jones, Lowell Jackson, Malik Parks, Darnell Mangum, Marcus Sivels, Ricky Edwards, Sr. My brothers from Morgan State were also visiting. On October 18th, eleven men and I crossed the Burning Sands into the Gamma Sigma Chapter of Alpha Phi Alpha Fraternity, Inc. The pressure was on, and I wasn't going to miss a beat.

I marched in the homecoming parade. After marching, I went off to perform my Neo duties for the BBQ on the Alpha plot. From there, I went to the band room to make sure my chapter and band were ready to meet and greet our visiting band. We marched to the stadium for the pre-game show, performed in the halftime show, then a 5th quarter battle of the bands after the game. After the game, we met with the visiting bands' chapter to sing the national hymn jointly, which today happens to be the chapter that wrote the national hymn, Eta Gamma, at the end of the night. This was my day to strive and show what it means to be a Hornet, a Man of Psi, and an Alpha Man! None of this would have been possible without the help and support of all my chapter brothers.

There comes a time in every bandsman career when they have their last undergrad performance. I'm proud to share my last time putting on that Columbia blue and red uniform. In January of 2009, DSU's band made history by becoming one of the few HBCU bands to perform for President Barack Obama's Inauguration. This was my final performance with the band before graduating in 2010. It was one of the most memorable and coldest parades I had ever marched in.

The sense of pride I felt as I marched down Pennsylvania Avenue, and looked to my right to see the first Black President, Barack Obama and First Lady Michelle Obama, was something I will never forget. As we played "American Boy" by Estelle, all I could think about was how much I loved my HBCU and how much I loved being a Hornet.

About Chevis Anderson

Chevis grew up in the Philadelphia Public School system. Where he attended Overbrook High School, where he joined the Jazz & Concert Bands and Performance Choir. Upon graduating from Overbrook High, Chevis Attend Delaware State University on a Music scholarship for Participation in the university Marching Band, better known as the Approaching Storm, where he later obtained his B.A. Degree in Music Business and a Minor in Broadcast Journalism from Delaware State University - May 2010.

In his Collegiate tenure, Chevis became a Brother of the Eta Psi Chapter of Kappa Kappa Psi National Honorary Band Fraternity, Inc., Spring 2003; a Brother Gamma Sigma Chapter of Alpha Phi Alpha Fraternity, Inc., Fall 2003; President of the NPHC DSU Chapter, 04/05; Student Senator for the College of Visual and Performing Arts, and his greatest highlight was his opportunity to March in the 2009 Inaugural Parade for President Barack Obama.

Currently, Chevis resides in Charlotte NC where he teaches Music and Owns a Media Entertainment Company.

Christopher Goins

The Machine that Saved My Life

Christopher Goins

North Carolina A&T State University

Depressed. Lonely. Suicidal.

Before I became a drum major for the Marching Machine, I was an isolated Black boy whose sexuality seemed like a death sentence.

I was born and raised in Greensboro, North Carolina, where my parents were unapologetic about their love for North Carolina Agricultural and Technical State University. Their love for the school trickled down to me. As a child, I set a goal to one day become the drum major for the Marching Machine. The drum major of any HBCU marching band is a coveted position in the community. Many people, like me, set a goal as a child to become that one day. My parents encouraged this dream by supporting my love for music, the band and playing the trumpet. They also realized that, for years, the best incentive to get me to do my chores and get rid of me every Saturday during football season was to purchase season tickets, just for me, at Aggie Stadium. Rain, sleet or snow, I attended the games—not to watch the football game—but to stalk Dr. Hodge (former Director of Bands); Dr. Kenny Ruff (former drum major and current Director of Bands); Anthony Criss (the drum major whom I thought walked on water); and the Marching Machine itself. When I was a senior in high school, I only applied to A&T because all I ever wanted was to one day be an Aggie. Unbeknownst to me, this adoration of the university and the Marching Machine would one day save my life.

As I got older, I became what is known as a "bandhead." I graduated from Dudley High School in 1996 with a deep sense of pride and accomplishment in my musical growth and development. My closest friends were also bandheads. We grew up together, emulating the Marching Machine. We were like brothers, and we all proudly joined the band at A&T. We set band goals for ourselves. We all planned to pledge Kappa Kappa Psi. I was going to be drum major, and they were going to be the best section leaders the band had ever seen, just like we did in high school! In fact, the Machine embraced us all. The Machine quickly saw our leadership potential and pure passion for the band.

Freshman year in the band was so much *fun*! Dr. Hodge realized that he had recruited an amazing class of freshmen, and he took the band on tour. Our Dudley crew was a clique of the cool kids who everyone loved, too. We were devastated when marching band season was over. Some of us joined the pep and symphonic band, but it wasn't the same. During the off-season, we spent our time dreaming about the upcoming season when A&T would travel to the Circle City Classic in Indianapolis. Everyone knew that I was poised to be the next drum major, and my crew was very protective of me. The off-season also gave me time to explore my sexuality. I secretly started dating other men. I felt sworn to secrecy because I had witnessed, and even sometimes participated in, the gossip and ridicule that a gay person received in my community. But I was having the time of my life. It was a secret I enjoyed keeping to myself.

Late in the spring of 1997, the crew came together for one of our weekly nighttime sessions at the Dudley stadium. This particular night was awkward and felt "off", mainly because someone had invited a person in the band who wasn't a part of our crew. I didn't like him too much because I always felt like he was a hater. I didn't say anything about it, but I didn't trust him. I noticed that this time wasn't like all the other times when we talked about our dreams in the band. Instead, we engaged in a lot of small talk. I noticed that the crew had shifted their positions to all focus on me.

I asked, "What's going on?"

My best friend at the time said, "Chris, we love you and we want to talk to you."

Then came the dreaded question that no 19-year-old young man wants anyone to ask: "Are you gay?"

I responded by saying, "I don't know. I kept those feelings away from you all because I'm still trying to figure things out." I admitted to seeing some guys they didn't know. I talked about other gay men who we knew and assured my crew that I wasn't like "them." I wasn't messy, feminine or trying to be a woman. I wanted my friends to know that there are gay men in the world who are not what they perceived as outcast or someone to be ashamed of. So, I honestly felt that the crew was learning from me and that this was a teachable moment.

My crew encouraged me to go to church. They told me not to be gay because it would hurt my quest to become drum major and it would hinder our chances of pledging Kappa Kappa Psi. Also, they were afraid of what people would say about their friendship with me and even assume that they were gay, too. Because this social circle was so important to me, I heeded their advice. I tried to "pray the gay away." I attempted to get a girlfriend and tried to be overly masculine. For a few weeks, things seemed to revert back to normal. However, the rumors exploded out of nowhere and people knew about my sexuality. I was horrified. But I could pinpoint that the "guest" in our last session was the one spreading the rumors.

I didn't want to be called a liar, so I answered the inquiries about my sexuality. My crew members were all disappointed in me and they made their separation from me public. (Thank God we didn't have social media back then!) Some of the women I had dated felt betrayed and their hurt fueled more gossip. The gay men I encountered in my secret life were either mad, wanted to ruin me, or became afraid that I would out them, too. They made their distance obvious, as well. I could not escape the questions and isolation. So, I prescribed to the narrative that I was not going to be a drum major, nor was I going to pledge Kappa Kappa Psi. I thought about suicide. I thought about quitting the band. I thought about relocating to another college. But, God!

When it was time for band camp in the fall of 1997, I missed my crew. I thought about how excited we would be leading up to the first day of camp. But this time was different. I reluctantly showed up and knew that the questions about me being gay were going to resurface. After the first 5 a.m. workout, Dr. Hodge called me over in front of the rest of his band staff. My heart sank. I honestly thought he was going to talk to me about the rumors. Instead, he said, "By 9 a.m., your head needs to be fucking bald because all of my drum majors look like me." I broke down in tears in front of him and his staff on my knees because he was telling me that I was going to be his next drum major. That mean, old man put his arm around me and said, "Son, it's going to be alright."

My band loved on me from that point on. They renewed my faith in friendship and fostered a new level of brotherhood when I later joined Kappa Kappa Psi. I went on to become chapter president. The protection I once felt from my crew was replaced by an army of brothers who loved Chris, the *authentic* Chris. My band family understood my pain, and they became vocal allies against those who ridiculed me.

This moment in the band at A&T helped define my leadership and how I have tried to foster safe spaces for Black students so that no one will ever feel the way I did. I protect the most vulnerable. This experience forced me to become the type of friend and mentor I needed then. It showed me how important community is and that isolation isn't healthy. I have committed myself to being like the brothers I gained in my fraternity. I am unapologetic about rooting for the underdog the way Dr. Hodge did for me. I have a profound sense of grace for others that will not allow anyone to be defined by a single mistake in their past, nor by someone else's fear and ignorance.

I have founded and led a high school for Black students on the south side of Chicago. Currently, I lead President Obama's My Brother's Keeper Initiative for Chicago so that all Black boys can experience a loving, restorative community like the Marching Machine of North Carolina A&T State University.

About Christopher Goins

F. Christopher Goins is currently the Chief Equity Officer for Thrive Chicago and charged with leading President Obama's My Brothers Keeper (Chicago) initiative, which is in partnership with the Obama Foundation. He is a passionate advocate for racial equity in education and has dedicated his professional career to closing the opportunity gap for black students. The former Founding Principal of Butler College Prep from 2013-2019, the school and Goins received national recognition as the number one public school in Illinois, serving black students, for its academic growth and for its ONESOUL initiative aimed at ending the 2% crisis of males of color in the teaching field. A native of Greensboro, NC, Goins is a graduate of North Carolina Agricultural and Technical State University (B.S. History/Secondary Education) and the University of Cincinnati (Masters of Urban Educational Leadership). In 2006, Goins was the youngest person selected to be Guilford County School's Teacher of the Year for his work as a Civics and AP Government and Politics teacher at James B. Dudley High School. Goins received the 2015 Mayor Rahm Emmanuel's Principal Achievement Award and Butler College Prep was highlighted as the highest performing high school, that serves African American students, in Chicago. In 2016, Chicago Magazine ranked Butler as the Top Charter High School in the city. Goins, is a member of Alpha Phi Alpha Fraternity, Incorporated and a 2016 Surge Fellow, the key initiative of the Surge Institute.

Keena Day

A Whole New World

Keena Day

Tennessee State University

In the fall of 1999, selected members of the Aristocrat of Bands from Tennessee State University performed for Stevie Wonder at the Grand Ole Opry in Nashville. In that moment hearing Stevie playing in the background before we marched into the venue, I remember thinking that this is where playing my euphonium had landed me-- a little girl from Detroit was performing for one of Detroit's most iconic musicians. TSU performed "Master Blaster" right in front of him; it was hard to contain my tears. For me and so many other young Black instrumentalists, marching in an HBCU band afforded us opportunities to see important people and visit places we may have never seen otherwise. I do not take that experience for granted.

Navigating the marching band world was a slight challenge for me because it was outside of what I knew music to be. Music has been a part of my life all of my life. My parents, grandfather, several aunts and uncles have all been professional musicians. I grew up with band practices in the basement of our home with instruments all over. Romantically, even all of the men I have ever loved including my husband were musicians. My sons are musicians. Music is an essential part of my life. It is hard to understand me or the people around me without understanding musical people. However, despite my musical background, marching band wasn't known to me until high school.

Outside of the norm in my family to play bass, guitar, or other string instruments, in third grade, I began playing trumpet. Having grown up in a family that performed jazz and popular music, I was determined to play like Dizzy Gillespie—the embodiment of trumpet playing to me with an embouchure that worked for him, but would do nothing for me, except become a burden.

Even though I attended neighborhood public schools that were heavily Black on the West Side of Detroit, both my elementary and middle school band teachers were white men. We played pep tunes like "Hail to the Victors", "Tequila", or "Go Big Blue", and with my facsimile Dizzy cheeks when I played, it wasn't until I attempted to play at Cass Technical High School that I learned there was much more to Black music than what I had been taught as a trumpet player.

Not only was Cass Tech a mecca for the best high school musicians to learn in the world-renowned symphonic and jazz programs, but it boasted a marching band that strictly followed the HBCU band tradition. I had never been in a marching band or heard the kind of music played. I'd also be the first in my immediate family to go to college; thus, the understanding of how to get into college or even the HBCU college marching traditions themselves were all new to me. In the "CTMB", I learned what a crab name was, what concert scales were, what a band challenge was, and the expectations of uniformity, sportsmanship, and unity. Under the direction of Ms. Sharon Allen, a Black band director who was an alumna of an HBCU marching band, she built a legacy of instrumentalists who were polished, articulate, and confident. We were groomed to be the absolute best in Detroit.

Immediately, I struggled due to my embouchure-- the easy and whitewashed tunes I played in middle school had not prepared me for the rigors of being in her band. She noticed that I had not been taught out of that bad playing habit and switched me to euphonium. She also made sure that as a female low brass player that I particularly knew that I needed to quickly learn if I was going to play a traditionally male instrument. She produced the top female brass and percussion musicians in the city, and I worked hard to be counted among them. Practicing became a regularity. The biggest impact she had on my musical development was that she took us to homecoming games at HBCUs in the South and challenged us to audition at every HBCU we could. I took heed; suddenly the dream of attending college at an HBCU was a reality for me and my family after I swept my scholarship auditions and had ten school options.

In making the decision of what school to attend, a few factors were at play for me. The most important of course was style and edge; I wanted to attend a school known for its musical arrangements and that the band had a distinct role for euphonium sections. The second factor was how accepted women were in the marching band without stigmas of sexism or patriarchal systems where women did not serve in leadership roles in the band. Those things in mind, I visited several schools with prominent programs my senior year. Tennessee State University became an early favorite. The band director, Edward L. Graves talked with me about women as musicians and leaders at TSU starting in the late 1970s and how he believed that TSU would be a place where I would excel as a player. TSU had an undeniable air of aristocracy that was palpable in band tapes and in person. Once Prof Graves got my parents on board, TSU became my choice.

I remember walking onto the campus of Tennessee State during the summer of 1999 as an engineering major and starting college in a summer program about three weeks after my high school graduation. During the summer program, any time I had free time from classes, I was in the band room "going to the woodshed" with the other freshmen male brass players vying to play for the Aristocrat of Bands-- I was determined to make 1st baritone as a freshman. TSU is known for its flare of using distinctly unique instruments—the trumpets even played "dizzy" shaped horns. That year, the section was shifting to the larger and much coveted marching euphoniums that fall; those horns were like literal monster trumpets. I was determined to pull my weight by knowing every single note that I could.

Not only did I make it in the section, but I also marched next to the section leader as a sort of grooming ritual for freshman standouts. The season was tough and grueling. But I loved playing and practicing. I always worked to improve my craft simply because as a woman, I always felt like I had more to prove. I would credit our band arranger, James "Dean" Sexton, with making me love the marching euphonium; he literally wrote music specifically for the powerful section the 1999 baritone section became. Songs like "Word Up", "Master Blaster", "Fantasy", and other distinct euphonium countermelodies that really were arranged specifically for the power and majesty of that section. We played in sync together on every march and technical piece-- the section was known as "Tone Patrol". With those beautiful marching euphoniums, we dominated as a section and ended that year winning "Best Section" of the AOB.

During my four years as a member of the AOB, we traveled extensively, performed in large Nashville events, performed for sports teams like the Nashville Predators and the Tennessee Titans (during the championship years of Steve McNair and Eddie George), and more. Dean continued to write charts specifically for the euphonium section that are iconic to the Aristocrat of Bands sound during that era. What's really fascinating about playing in an HBCU college band is that beyond the members of the AOB whom became close as family, was the friendly camaraderie among HBCU bands. TSU played schools like FAMU, Jackson St and a few others. As chapters of musical fraternities Phi Mu Alpha, Sinfonia and Sigma Alpha Iota began to emerge within HBCUs, we all made it our business to fellowship. From those connections, we would come together and discuss our bouts such as the infamous Grambling versus TSU game in Las Vegas. Honda Battle of the Bands (from which TSU participated in the inaugural year in 2003) became a family reunion of sorts for musicians at HBCUs. We created events yearly just to stay connected after we became alumni. Though we marched in competing bands, we became family. Many of those people are still remarkably close to me to this day, and we support each other through every life event.

I always continued to play in jazz ensembles and symphonic bands throughout my secondary and collegiate matriculations. Despite my wholehearted love of jazz and classical music, marching band opened up my world and created a nostalgia of not only musicality and prowess as a low brass player, but also the presence of friends and outstanding Black music instructors which wasn't how I started my journey as a musician. What I learned was that representation of seeing what you aspire to be in another person, not being afraid of high expectations, and pushing your knowledge beyond fear can shape your life beyond your wildest dreams. HBCU bands gave that to me.

About Keena Day

Keena Day is an educator, writer and poet. She is currently the Senior Manager of Humanities grades 6-12 for DSST Public Schools, after serving as the Director of Secondary Literacy grades 5-12 for KIPP: Colorado Schools, and a Moonshot Fellow (Fall 2019). Prior to COVID-19 mass closures of schools, Keena worked with The Colorado Department of Education to evaluate bias and access for 5th and 6th grade state assessments. She has been an educator for 17 years; Keena has taught grades 6-12, AP Language and AP Literature and at the collegiate level as an adjunct freshman composition and technical writing instructor. Keena leads school leadership, teachers, and school organizations in many areas of literacy including curriculum, assessment, instructional design, leadership coaching, data analysis, systematic programming implementation, and literacy best practices. Keena is a trained literacy specialist and coach, and is a National Association of Advanced Teacher Education (NAATE) alumna Keena is also a freelance writer and journalist writing for several media outlets such as the Tennessee Tribune, Boardhawk, and My Black Colorado Magazine. She is the author of two books: AFROdisiacs (2019) and The Colors of My Boudoir (2020). She has been a guest on podcasts and radio shows and has been a speaker at conferences focused on Black women's empowerment, education, and literacy instruction. Keena hails from Detroit, MI where she was educated at the world-renowned Cass Technical High School; she received her B.A., and M.A., in English with education credentials from Tennessee State University where she served as a section leader of the Aristocrat of Bands. Keena serves on the Board of Commissioners for the Diversity, Equity and Inclusion commission for Commerce City, Colorado and is a board member of the Colorado Women for Political Action (CBWPA), a board member of NOW!, Inc., where she serves as Executive Director, a board member of Boss Generation, Inc., a committee chairwoman for The Poetry Society of Colorado and is president of the Tennessee State University Colorado Alumni Chapter. Keena was recognized as a "Forty Under 40" Awardee for TSU's 2020 class and selected as one of the top 100 educators in Colorado by My Black Colorado Magazine. Keena is currently a Doctoral student in Organizational Leadership at the University of Dayton. She is the mother of two sons and currently resides in Denver.

Kelton J. Penson

Don't Break Records: Set the Standard

Kelton J. Penson

Texas Southern University

"B-I-G P-O-P-P-A, no info for the DEA…" This was one of the many 1997 summer jams and "man did it". It was a hot, sunny Sunday in August, around 5 p.m. in the "Third Ward". We pulled up to the corner of Cleburne and Ennis. To the left of us was the ninth wonder of the world, Thee Texas Southern University Ocean of Soul Marching Band Room! As we parked, there were several young teens, eager to become young adults via The Ocean migrated in the band parking lot. You could tell who knew each other and who played what. The drummers walked around with sticks. Tuba players had mouthpieces. Dancers were dressed all pretty. As the start of the freshmen meeting drew closer, we heard things get quiet. We did not know what to expect. We were there to get information, and to meet the band director and staff.

Let's travel back to Jack Yates High School, where this all started. Ninth grade was the hardest time of my life. Perseverance was the teacher of this lesson. What I thought I knew, I did not! Growing up seeing Yates Band Director "Mrs. T" (RIP) lead that band, I knew I wanted to be a Lion. Her style of leading and giving back as a Black woman and doing it with pride, was appreciated. She cared about us sincerely. To our surprise, the first day of band camp, she met with the band and announced her transition to Willowridge. We would be under the leadership of Professor Edward Jackson.(RIP) We all were shocked. In the tenth grade, I had an opportunity to audition for TSU by Professor John Henry. Professor Jackson taught us, "Don't pass up free money!"

I played what I had prepared at that moment, and I received a rating of 1. This was the moment of truth. We really were not pushing the TSU envelope because we were bred to go to "The BOX."

Since me and my best bud Renferd Joseph were two of Houston's most-wanted, I told Ren, "Man, wherever we go, we just need to wake up and show up!" As we advanced in high school studies, we were met with another obstacle. We were now under a new Director of Bands, Mr. Darryl Williams (PV) during our junior year. Professor Jackson took a job back home in Mississippi. With this change came new opportunities. Mr. Williams was very instrumental with getting us auditions at Prairie View A&M University. By now, the "two boys from Yates" were the talk of the town. Everyone wanted to know where we were going. We moved in a pack! It was time to visit PV!

I, Ren and Mr. Williams drove to PV on a Saturday to meet Professor George Edwards (RIP) and Professor Larry Jones. Professor Jones was ecstatic to have us come, for he felt he had landed the big plane. Arriving in front of Hobart, our nerves set in! This was a long time coming. To us, this was the Mecca of Drums. Developed relationships with old heads and, learning from current players, vibes were racing through our veins. Both directors greeted us. We spoke back, sounding like little wimps.

After Professor Jones finished praising us and telling Prof Edwards "These are the two I was telling you about," Professor Edwards paused. He looked over his glasses and said, "Hell, I need to hear y'all play something! I'm not spending any money and I ain't heard a thing!" Professor Jones went to get a drum. Our eyes lit up. We were about to play on a "BLUE". Professor started playing the fast march, which was used to transition the band to dance block. He asked us to play it back and we murdered it!

"Okay, take them upstairs!" Professor Edwards said. Me and Ren were like, "Is that it? Favor!" We sat down with everyone in charge and commenced to talk business. That's when the screen "Fades to Black." Senior year was fast approaching, and we needed to solidify our college experience.

Things did not go as planned for us at PV, and we were a little disappointed. This was one of our burning desires. We had a promising future in The Box. There were only two spots open for snare that upcoming year. Me and Ren were coming for it! While traveling back to Houston, I asked Ren for his cell phone to call the TSU band office. Mrs. Hunter answered the phone. I told her it was KP from Yates, and I asked to be connected with Mr. Lee. The first thing he asked was, "Have you come to a decision?"

"Guess what? We are on the way!" I responded!

"We?" he asked.

"We are leaving PV now heading back to Yates…"

"Well, I will see you guys when you get here!"

As we proceeded toward TSU band hall to sign the line, I asked Ren, once more, "Dawg, you sure?"

He replied, "School is about to start. We need to get in somewhere!"

We signed!

Our senior year was ending. Friends started receiving offers and making plans to move out of state. Many people asked us, "Where y'all going?"

"TSU!" we replied!

We chose The Ocean over The Storm. It did not make sense to many at first because everyone knew we wanted to march in The Box. Many schools took ideas and cadences, went back to their perspective schools, and imitate to the best of their abilities. I shared this with REN.

"Why go to an already established drum section where we will only be two more cold dudes in The Box, at best? Let's go to TSU and build a bridge and provide access for the future!"

I was thankful for the opportunity Mr. Lee gave us to display our gifts. He allowed us to bring to fruition what is now known as one of the most versatile drum sections on the planet. During our first year in the band, we overcame several obstacles. "Take that back down 290!" was one of the most recited lines from old heads who knew us! We got called out for everything. We just played through it. Yes, it was an adjustment. We were now playing on plastic heads, drums tuned much lower, just trying to adjust to TSU's style of play. After completing our freshman year, Ren and I had the honor of leading the drum section our second year in the band. We brought in more awareness of the culture to help us remain competitors in this industry and keep the organization afloat. At this point, we knew our gifts were making room for us! We caught more hell from the old heads!

It was not until later that the old heads really started to see that we were not there to change the book, but to enhance it. During the 99' marching season, only three snares survived: Me, Ren and Matthew Ford. We were trying to get Matt to march tenor. He said, "Nope! We need at least three."

The games were a little different now though! "Texas Southern 3 Snares" was the hot topic on 5th Quarter and The SWAC page. We did our job that year in supporting the band with a beat. But when it came down to snare battles, Matt let me and Ren loose. The accolades received were phenomenal. We witnessed the tables turn and we heard The Funk Train become a household name. The 2000 season was one for the books, I must say. We didn't break records! We set more standards! We were blessed to serve one of the best class of rookies since we took charge. The level of excellence in achievement had arrived. We felt timing was right to concentrate on our degrees.

Prayer, relationships and preparation were essential in my success at Texas Southern. The lifelong relationship that myself and Ren maintain demonstrates to others how the vision plus the gifts of help always equal a win! I am now Director of Bands at Lawson Academy, Lead percussionist at Higher Dimension Church and Percussion Coach at Texas Southern University. My prayer is for the youth to take the seed sown, finish the job and be a proud alum of Thee Texas Southern University or the institution of choice!

Remember

#OnlyThePreparedProceed

About Kelton J. Penson

As an avid lover of music, Kelton J. Penson had dreamed of becoming an educator since he was 12 years old. His love of music started at a young age, having grown up playing drums in church. His leadership role has always been noticed, while in middle school band he was placed over the drum section and served as lead percussionist. After graduating from middle school and transitioning to high school, Kelton was determined to be a part of the best band in the land, "THEE REV.JACK YATES SENIOR HIGH SCHOOL", Marching Motion Band, where he would study under some of the best DIRECTORS OF BANDS, and yet again be BLESSED to co-lead THE BEST SECTION IN HOUSTON, (T.O.P). During the next four years of Kelton's life, he understood that those years were very imperative for the next steps of his life. Kelton was very active in his high school years, being involved in MARCHING, CONCERT BANDS, VARIOUS SOCIAL CLUBS, and a host of other organizations on and off campus. While completing his high school studies, Kelton auditioned for Texas Southern University during his 10th grade year where he received a full scholarship. With a passion for music, Kelton kept striving to be the best he could. Upon graduating from high school, he chose to attend the prestigious University of TEXAS SOUTHERN where he would study MUSIC EDUCATION and become a member of the OCEAN OF SOUL, under the direction of Richard F. Lee. As a result of accepting the offer to be a member of the University and band program, Kelton's entire life was on the brink of a "Life of Promise". Through his innovative and unique approach to obtaining his degree, he pushed himself to reach his goals every day. "HARDWORKER". During his second year in band, Kelton was awarded the title of leading the "Most Versatile Drum Section" in the land better known as "The FunkTrain" alongside of Renferd Joseph. With a burning desire to save, educate and advance music in the minds of future musicians, the two of these young men opened the door for many others to travel down that same road of success that was being offered through education at TxSU. The turnout was record-breaking, and sparked Kelton's passion for education on the next level. Several fraternities were discovered while in attending TSU. Some included RHO CHI PSI (spr98)- "Recruitment and Retention organization, PHI MU ALPHA (spr01) "Professional Music Frat". Kelton graduated from Texas Southern in the top percent of his class in 2003. Today, he is working in education for THE LAWSON ACADEMY- music educator, Texas Southern University Band- Percussion Coach, and Higher Dimension Church – lead drummer (22yrs).

Stanley Holloway

When I Shed My Skin: A Rattler's Experience in the Marching "100"

Stanley Holloway

Florida A&M University

The drum major called the band to attention after six distinct blown whistles with a slight pause in between each two.

"Band... Atten—hut!"

We didn't hear anything from the band, except the sound of their feet driving into the ground and the swift movement of their capes and uniforms. The drum major blew another six distinct whistles and commanded the band to start the show.

"Hey... Hey... Hey... Yo... Good evening, ladies and gentlemen! From the highest of seven hills in Tallahassee, the capital of Florida, please welcome what has become known as 'America's Band'. The incomparable... magnificent... the number 1 band in the country. The Florida... A&M... University... Marching Band! But first... the sound!"

When you see this band and hear this commentary, be prepared to be amazed at the showmanship, creativity and musicianship of the Florida A&M University Marching "100" band.

I was absolutely in love with this band ever since I saw them live for the first time when I was six years old in 1986 vs. Southern University. They did a sports hall of fame show that I will never forget. There were formations of a stick-man figure hitting a baseball and shooting a basketball. They also made a formation of a track shoe and a football. Even as a child, I recognized everything they did with the formations and the music they played, such as the *Harlem Globe Trotters Theme* and *Take Me Out to the Ball Game*. At the time, I watched them in complete awe. They appeared to be giants in my eyes. Little did I know, eventually, I'd attend Florida A&M as a

student and join the ranks of the Marching "100" where I stood on the shoulders of those giants.

I had an unforgettable experience in the Marching "100" from the time I set foot on campus for pre-drill in August 2000 until the time I completed my academic journey as a student and left the hill. My eyes were opened to many things that I was oblivious to before joining this great organization, in addition to being a part of a culture within the HBCU band world. I would have never experienced it had I not joined the band at FAMU.

What's A Crab?

Eventually, I made the decision, which I thought would be the obvious choice, to attend Florida A&M University and join the band. It wasn't until the summer of 2000 at band camp, two years after I graduated high school, that I decided to go to school in Tallahassee. Although a few times during my matriculation at FAMU, I wondered what my life would have been like if I went elsewhere, but I do not regret making this decision. On day one of pre-drill, all freshmen, sections leaders and band officers were to report. The upperclassmen were to report the following week. I thought this would be a continuation of band camp where everything was positive and jovial. But that was quickly dispelled. I had some uncomfortable encounters and teachable moments that made me think to myself, *What have I gotten myself into?*

I went to audition on the third floor of the Foster-Tanner music building. This is where I met most of my freshman sisters, even though I met some of them at band camp. We all seemed to come together at this moment. At FAMU, we never referred to anyone as a "crab" as some other bands do. You were just a freshman with your freshman sisters and brothers. From that first encounter, they were to become my sisters for life! Our bond is as

strong now long after that first day at pre-drill, and it will never diminish! For some reason, we all were nervous for this audition, even though it was the same as it was at band camp.

What if they send us home? we all thought.

"Well, I didn't come to school here just to bomb an audition only to get sent back home," I thought. So, it was my turn for the audition, and I started sweating! I walked in the room and there was the Director of Piccolos, along with the Section Leader and Assistant Section Leader sitting across from each other. While I was walking in, they were all smiling, laughing and having a good ole time. Then, the minute I entered everything stopped. The air got thin, and they had the straightest face I have ever seen in unison!

Oh, boy! I see how this going to go, I thought.

"I'm sure you know what you need to do and play for me right?" she said.

"Yes, ma'am," I said. I started playing all of my major and minor scales, chromatic with all relative octaves, and audition etudes. I then played two marches, "Rolling Thunder" and "Them Basses".

"Young man, don't you want to play something else?" she asked.

I knew exactly what she wanted to hear, but I answered, "No, ma'am. I believe I played everything."

"Well, I highly suggest you play the piccolo solo from Stars and Stripes," she said.

With much hesitation, I just flat out told her I didn't know it, at least the version that had been played for decades at FAMU. I fumbled through it at band camp and had only played the orchestra version in high school, which was in a totally different key signature.

"You need to play something," she said.

So, I started playing the orchestra version, which was still awfully bad. After I played, she stared at me and all three of them looked at each other. She made some kind of mark on my audition paper and told me to wait outside. I just knew I was going home. I had already started planning in my head how I was going to get back home without calling my mom.

Did I Make It?

It was 7 p.m. at the start of orientation for everyone. There were approximately 180 freshmen, plus section leaders and officers. Little did I know that there were another 200 members who were going to show up the following week. At this point in the night, it was safe to assume that I wasn't being sent home.

The first part of the night was a lot of talking and presentations that I don't remember. I was bored.

"When are we going to play?" I kept asking myself. When we finally did play, we played a lot of music for the remainder of the rehearsal! I was pushed to my max musically and quickly learned that "Perfection of Musicianship" was not just something we said in the band motto. It was taken very seriously. It was the standard of excellence for all members to follow.

Although it seemed difficult and mentally exhausting as a freshman, it was just a humble start to a phenomenal journey I had in the Marching "100". I experienced some great moments that cannot be erased. They will forever be a part of my history. I remember being fitted for a uniform and wearing it. I remember the first home game and performance at Bragg Stadium, when we played SCSU in Jacksonville, Florida for the first away game. I got to perform against my peers whom I had went to school with previously. I remember the first time I performed in front of 50,000 plus fans at the Atlanta Classic vs. Tennessee State University, what went down in history as an intense battle against Southern University and, arguably, the most epic Florida Classic halftime performance from both bands in history against Bethune-Cookman.

My freshman year in the Marching "100" was unforgettable. It paved the way for me to continue my legacy within the organization. I finally shed my skin and was able to become a venomous rattler, where I later went on to become the assistant section leader of the piccolos my sophomore and junior year. I became co-section leader my senior year, and additionally became a member of the Delta Iota Chapter of Kappa Kappa Psi National Honorary Band Fraternity Incorporated in the spring of 2002. The years following my arrival on the hill were equally exciting and memorable in which I was able to expand socially and meet more individuals across the HBCU band world. Through these encounters, I was able to build lifelong friendships and alliances, both personally and professionally. My experience at Florida A&M University and with the Marching "100" was my experience and mine alone. Although there may be some similarities, and some relatable moments among my peers, when the dust clears after the rattler cadence and sequence on the patch, my experience stands alone.

Highest Quality of Character

Achievement in Academics

Attainment in Leadership

Perfection in Musicianship

Precision in Marching

Dedication to Service

About Stanley Holloway

Stanley "Stan" Holloway was born in 1980 in Columbia, South Carolina. Growing up, he was fascinated with music, and this interest led to some early exposure to an instrumental focus since he was drawn to the joy of music. Later, Mr. Holloway, who now teaches woodwind techniques at the college level, developed a passion for the ideas and creativity behind music. Stan completed a bachelor's degree from Florida A&M University in 2005 while being involved in numerous activities and organizations such as the Florida A&M University Marching "100" band. Where he served as the piccolo section assistant section leader for 2 years and Co-Section Leader for 1 year during his 4 year tenure. Additionally, he further provided service and cultivated a wholesome band experience to the band program through Kappa Kappa Psi National honorary band fraternity inc.

Stan resides in Jacksonville Florida with his wife Shannon and daughter Samone. Due to the current pandemic, Stan choses to stay at home with his family where they continue at home education for his child and manage and own a transportation dispatch service. Stan also arranges and composes music for various music ensembles, creative drill writing for marching bands, provides private lessons for students ranging from middle school to college and creates electronic music for video games and commercials. Mr. Holloway also works as the Assistant Director and Woodwind Instructor for the Edward Waters College Triple Threat Marching Band.

Recently, Mr. Holloway has completed a Bachelor of Science degree from Full Sail University in Music Production, a master's degree in Music Education from Liberty University completing a thesis project on *"Creating A Music Education Curriculum Based on Current Teaching Strategies"* and now continuing his education as he pursues a Doctorate in Music Education while continuously researching for his dissertation on how black males can influence elementary music education. Because of his love for music and mentoring, Stan is dedicated to helping students experience the soulful joy of music making by energizing their passion for the arts, fundamentals, and of course, having fun!

Stephen Edgerton

Everlasting Influence
Stephen Edgerton

Winston Salem State University
North Carolina Central University

"Well," she said in a tone of conclusion. "All your stuff is packed. If everything is good and on the up, I'll leave you. If not, you'll just have to come home and do something else." My mother's words resonated in my head. But I didn't want to come home. I was optimistic. I was ecstatic because I was *wanted*. I went from not expecting to go to college at all to feeling like a top draft pick headed to my team.

Winston Salem State University was where I was headed, and I didn't plan on returning. Upon arrival, the band director met us with a smile and personally escorted us around campus. I dropped my things off and, after a sentimental goodbye to my mother, I hardly unpacked before dressing and heading to what was left of band camp. It was the last week before school started. This is how my college journey began. No formal plans or agendas. Just jumping out on hope and motivation. A choice that would define my life.

My time at WSSU was truly a definitive start in the learning process of the complex culture of HBCU band life. I remember entering the band hall with my fresh new T-shirt and black shorts, which is what the practice uniform consisted of. I had already begun feeling unity, if only in appearance alone. There were a myriad of faces greeting me. Some excited, some with grins of approval, and some with a confounded, "Who's this guy?" expression. I had already slightly made a name for myself attending a summer music camp there. A good impression that left some current members hoping for my return. But I wasn't cocky. I knew I was in a new arena with new rules and new people. I was still a freshman in all senses of it. I armed myself only with confidence in my ability and an internal excitement for the unknown. I caught on fast and always knew my music. Most of all, I humbled myself to seniority. If you didn't, you learned pretty fast that you weren't special.

The sousaphone section was known as the "Fiberglass Foolz". This was partly because of the material of the instrument previously and the persona the section carried due to crazy antics and unpredictable behavior. There were seven other freshmen with me, including my best friend in life and two "old heads". The group of us learned to do everything in sequence and together. We ate together, we arrived together, and we left practice together. This connection transferred to almost every aspect of band. Other sections were also like this: a family within a family and a bond within a bond. Nevertheless, I seemed to stick out, to the point the senior leaders decided to promote me to section leader. This was usually unheard of that a freshman would be chosen. I was one of the first. In this position, I received yet more diverse reactions. Some encouraging, some not so much. Still, not many could deny I was the person for the job. I can remember the first game. All ten of us lined up, with fresh uniforms and shiny, freshly polished silver sousaphone bells gleaming. Time seemed frozen until that funky drum cadence reverberated in my chest. It was showtime.

From marching in, to halftime, to marching out, it's game on all day. It often felt like we were in the middle of a battle and the other band was the enemy. In our mind, the football game served as a break between performances, not the other way around. One of my fondest memories is the night we played North Carolina A&T. My older brother attended A&T and was a F horn player and prominent arranger. We were badly outnumbered. Yet, looking across the field at him, both of us in uniform and well known to our prospective schools, it was the first time I felt like we were on the same plane. I wasn't the little brother. I was another warrior, ready to do battle.

After my freshman year, for different reasons, I transferred home to Durham, North Carolina and attended North Carolina Central University. It was a difficult transition, partly because, in my heart, I was still a Ram. I felt like I was betraying my first band family. They had become brothers and sisters. Such a bond had developed that it seemed painful to break. HBCU band life is that deep. But it was the right decision, no matter how difficult. Arriving that first day of practice, it was almost a replay of my first year. Some had heard of me. Some stared with a look of approval. Some wondered who the new guy was. I approached the same: humble and congenial, only showing up with my skills and openness, especially in the changing of styles and traditions.

I think the definitive game for me was playing against my former school. I remember being in the stands, watching them march in across the stadium. Everything was so familiar. I was almost doing the chants and movements in my seat, but I caught myself. I was in a different army now. When halftime came, I received the biggest shock that again impressed upon me the culture of HBCUs and bands. We had to enter the field for our halftime show on the visitor side. We went over early to get in place. As I lined up in my position, I expected to hear nasty remarks about being a traitor or the enemy. It was the opposite. So many of the fans who recognized me applauded and cheered me on, letting me know that, regardless, I was still a part of them. I was still *family*. It was an overwhelming feeling, one that I wasn't ready for.

After my first year of marching at NCCU, my director approached me about becoming drum major and leading the band. I was very hesitant, partly thinking I would be contributing less than I was as an instrumentalist. After a deep, stern lesson on leadership and influence, out of respect and obedience, I agreed. The difference in position was definitely a learning curve. All eyes are *always* on the drum major. You are the voice and vessel between the band director and the band. The drum major was as popular on campus as the quarterback. Drum major duties vary from HBCU to HBCU. For some, their responsibilities may be more on game day than throughout the week, depending on staff and assistance. Others have specific roles and responsibilities. In my position, it was all on me.

My band director entrusted me most days to carry out the mission and ensure the band followed schedule. Sometimes, he gave me the instructions on a note card before practice since he wouldn't be present for a few days, taking care of budget issues or administrative things. I was thrust into a great amount of leadership, and failure wasn't an option. In those years, I learned a great deal about communication, dealing with those from the sharpest to the dullest of intelligence. I developed empathy on a large scale for people of different experiences and backgrounds. I made it a point to learn where every member was from and to connect past a band level.

Besides the music and marching, I memorized flag and dance routines, as well as the cycles of drum cadences. I wanted to know every aspect that I was in charge of to maintain competence. I was their leader. I assured them that no one had their back like me. I assured them that they could be confident in whatever direction I led them. That, to me, was a drum major. Nothing brings it home like that walk out on the fifty-yard line on game day. The announcer was boosting the crowd energy. The stadium was loud with cheering. For those few seconds, nothing happened until I made it happen. The crowd was waiting on me. The band was waiting on me. Everything about me had to be deliberate.

There was so much preparation for seemingly eight minutes of glory during halftime. Eight minutes often felt like eight hours. Over twenty years later, the thought still brings goosebumps. Those experiences have served me well and prepared me in ways I never thought for a 20+ year career in the Army band field. The similarities were uncanny, and they allowed me to enter serving with leadership principles already in place. I also came to recognize that most of my Army band colleagues had nowhere near the experiences and cultural fervor that I had. The stories I told often produced inquisitive eyes and envious responses. Many recognized that I had a different pride that wasn't military produced in my performing. For me, the uniform was different. The mission was different. But the underlying principles still remained the same.

HBCU band was, is, and forever will be life. And its influence is everlasting.

About Stephen Edgerton

SSG Stephen Edgerton is a native of Durham, NC. He started his college studies at Winston Salem State University in 1993 becoming one of the band's very first freshman section leaders on tuba. He then transferred to North Carolina Central University to finish his college studies. He graduated in 1998 with a BA in Music. While at NCCU he served three years as drum major of the Sound Machine Marching Band. He also became a member of the Zeta Sigma Chapter of Kappa Kappa Psi National Honorary Band Fraternity where he served as historian and Vice President. Upon graduating, Stephen joined the military as an Army Bandsman. Currently serving in his 22nd yr, he has performed in over 15 countries to include a 12 month deployment to Bagdad, Iraq. He currently holds the position of drum major and senior bassist in the 82nd Airborne Division Band and Chorus in Fort Bragg, NC.

Terri L. White

Bigger Than Band
Terri L. White
Howard University

I didn't grow up around HBCU culture. I had heard the name "Grambling" because one of their alums brought the concept of "high stepping" to Pittsburgh. I marched in a high school program that I later learned was started by a FAMU graduate, but it never dawned on me that our whole schtick was distilled from the legacy of HBCU showbands. I eventually found myself in band camp at Howard University three weeks before classes started, mentally asking God what I had done to forsake Him to find myself thrown into a group of crazy people who thought running before the sun rose and treating band like the military were reasonable activities. Nonetheless, I persevered and enjoyed four amazing years as a clarinetist in the "Showtime" Marching Band and other university ensembles.

Being in band afforded me the opportunity to meet people from all over the country and travel to cities I had only ever read about. I developed better discipline, negotiation techniques, cooperation and leadership skills that would have been hard fought for without the structure and protocols that HBCU band culture demands. As life takes me further away from my years as an active performer, I find that the moments that hold the most powerful place in my memories aren't usually focused on football games or the grueling pace of learning new shows every week. Instead, I reflect on the lifelong friendships I developed through the years that were certainly rooted in our mutual participation in band but have continued to blossom into a family of sorts that I couldn't imagine my life without. I still reminisce about the thrill of hearing the addictive sound of a crowd cheering for you after a job well done. However, the moments that mean the most to me are those when I realized all of the hard work and dedication put into performances can bring joy to complete strangers.

My freshman year started in the fall of 2001 and by week three of the season, Showtime was slated to perform at a Canadian Football League game. The unthinkable happened the Tuesday before the trip as news reports covered plane crashes in New York, just outside of Pittsburgh and Washington. I still remember watching the smoke rise from the Pentagon with about a dozen dorm mates in our study lounge, a moment that will be etched in my mind forever. While everyone else was figuring out how to move forward, Showtime was one of the first student organizations to resume activities. We had an upcoming game against Morgan State in Baltimore and a home game against FAMU the following week. Gobs of students came to watch our practices during those weeks. For many, I imagine we were the only sense of normalcy they had while the university figured out next steps. By the FAMU game, I was exhausted from the stress of school, band and processing the historic event that had just happened. At the end of the game, I heard familiar voices calling my name: my godmother had brought her grandchildren down to surprise me and expose them to an HBCU football game. I remember running up to them and giving everyone big hugs, ready to vent about my experiences when they all started shouting at me.

"Man, I loved when you all played Just My Imagination! That is one of my favorite songs!"

"*Did you see those drummers!* I am gonna be a drummer like that when I get big!"

"Nah, man. I'm gonna play that big silver thing. Terri, what is that? They were getting it!"

"I wanna meet the dancers. Can I say hi to them? They were soooo pretty! Grandma, did you see their outfits?"

"You mean you get to do this *every week?!*"

It was in this moment that I knew my complaining would only have dampened the mood. When they watched us, all they saw was magic. I was still tired, annoyed, (and by then super hungry) but

I had never been prouder of myself and my fellow band members as I listened to those closest to me reenact their favorite parts of the day.

Years later, I found myself a junior in college, serving as clarinet section leader and vice president of my Tau Beta Sigma chapter. Howard's infamous coach bus provider delivered us to our performance late again, leaving little time to change, warm up or tune before we needed to march into the stadium. That Saturday found us playing against North Carolina A&T, the only crowd that ever gave my boisterous band competition when it came to heckling and cracking jokes. Personally, I was worried about an essay I had to write, stressed about an unfaithful boyfriend, and was overall annoyed with everything and everyone. We lined up ready to play Knights, Showtime's signature entrance song since at least the mid-1980s and decided to throw me angry, frustrated energy into my feet and instrument. The crowd surrounded us as we made our way into the stands. They didn't get in the way, but they certainly inspected us up close and personal to figure out what kind of band battle they were in store for. Toward the end of the song, I noticed a little girl jumping up and down, pointing at us. Next to her was a woman who I assumed to be her mother who simply laughed and smiled at her. As fate would have it, the clarinets were stopped in front of this little girl after the piece completed while the front end of our parade formation settled into their seats.

"Mommy, mommy look! They play clarinet, just like me! They look so grown up! I'm gonna be in the band just like them!"

Breaking all protocols, the fifteen or so clarinetists looked at her, smiled and waved. We asked how long she had been playing, encouraged her to keep it up, and to told her to go to Howard. In that instant, I was reminded of why I still enjoyed being a part of the craft, even if it wasn't always fun or easy. That game was one of the few performances I remember vividly. I hope that little girl could see the clarinets in both bands and that she was having a good time. She truly reminded me that the honor to be in the band was not a selfish act and it helped me check my own poor attitude for the day.

Fast forward to 2012. President Barack Obama was gearing up for what would become his second term in office. By then, I had left the D.C. area and was back in my hometown, taking care of my grandmother who had been diagnosed with dementia. Like many elders, she had a framed picture of the Obamas and was thrilled to see them in the White House. Talking about them was one of her favorite things to do. One day, I told her that I happened to have performed in front of Barack Obama before. As an alumna, I helped fill out the ranks of the band so that they could look more robust on television during the 2009 Inauguration Parade. Naturally, my grandmother didn't believe me. I pulled out my phone (my little computer as she called it) and showed the C-SPAN footage of Showtime in the parade. When the last row of instrumentalists (all clarinets) was on camera, I pointed myself out. After five views for confirmation, you would have thought I won the Nobel Peace Prize. Her voice got shaky, and she teared up, which was unusual for my normally spicy, sharp tongued grandmother. She went on about how proud she was of me. and asked me to replay it probably thirty more times, laughing and dancing in her seat to the music. From that moment forward, when her friends called, she would tell them, "My grandbaby played for the President!" and would fuss if they complained that they already knew. "Well, when *your* grandkids meet Obama, you can tell me a hundred times and I'll let you, so you are just gonna have to listen to me!"

Even as her condition worsened before her eventual passing, playing that clip was a sure-fire way to calm her down or cheer her up. By that point, that parade was far in my past but seeing her reaction knowing that her own family was a part of it was the best feeling ever.

Moments like these, from someone who came only upon the culture by chance, made every moment I spent in an HBCU band worth it. They remind me of the transformative nature the arts have on people and society. Most importantly, they have inspired me to bring a little bit of that "magic" to every aspect of my life ever since.

About Terri L. White, MBA

Terri L. White, MBA is a product strategist, award winning philanthropist and arts advocate, and entrepreneur. After years in a successful finance and museum fundraising career, she pivoted industries and currently works in supply chain technology for a major US retailer. Although she dabbled in various percussion and woodwind instruments Terri's primary musical talent lies with the clarinet, which she began playing at the age of seven. While studying communications and business at Howard University she participated in the marching, pep, and concert bands and was initiated into Tau Beta Sigma National Honorary Band Sorority, Incorporated. She holds additional degrees from George Mason University and the University of Pittsburgh. Thanks to her dedication to and advocacy for diversity and representation in the arts and humanities, she has won two 40 Under 40 Awards (2017 from Pittsburgh Magazine and 2019 from The Pittsburgh Courier) and a 20 Year Service Award from the Pittsburgh Symphony Orchestra in 2019. Ever committed to community service, Terri is an active member of Alpha Kappa Alpha Sorority, the Junior League, and her own service project initiatives centered around the elderly, adult literacy, and topics involving urban development and health.

Currently living in Charlotte with her dog and a bevy of huge houseplants, Terri is the Founder and President of Sugar Top Spirit & Beverage Co. According to the North Carolina Distillers' Association, once she commercially releases her first product (a blended bourbon with a planned Fall 2022 release date), she will be the first African American to own a commercial distillery in the state of North Carolina. You can connect with her on Twitter and Instagram @TerriWhite412.

Dr. Thomas L. Jones, Jr.

Stronger Than Adversity

Dr. Thomas L. Jones, Jr.

Hampton University

So, there I was, sitting in my containerized housing unit in full body armor, listening intently. In ideal cases, you might hear the alarm with enough time to run for cover. Other times, you hear the explosions first. In the latter case, you pretty much have to hope and pray that you're not one of the unlucky ones.

The klaxon blared, followed by the automated voice of, "Incoming! Incoming! Incoming!" IDF, or indirect fire, was a constant threat while stationed on Contingency Operating Base (COB) Basrah, in Iraq, late 2009. Mortars, rockets, and other projectiles were launched indiscriminately and haphazardly by insurgents just a few miles away, with the intent of inflicting battle damage and impacting morale. At best, IDF attacks are an inconvenience, but when it's bad, it's bad. Such was the case with three guys—Wertish, Drevnick, and Wilcox, ages 20, 22, and 27, respectively—who were simply in the wrong place at the wrong time. Out for a smoke break, they didn't even have time to hear the IDF alarm.

Gone. Just like that.

We live our lives, hoping to be better, to be great. For many of us, our goal is to impart on those we care about something lasting, enduring, and beneficial. We spend countless hours on training, education, and just experiencing the world in order to gain a sense of wisdom and insight that allows our voice to be heard amid the cacophony of abundant available information. For all our hopes and dreams, efforts and toils, The Great Equalizer can take it all from us—*permanently*.

If HBCU band life teaches us nothing else, it's that we are made stronger through adversity. In fact, research shows that those who endure an adverse initiation, ritual, or rite of passage in order to become a member of an organization, will appreciate that organization and ideals to a greater extent than simply being admitted to the organization on little to no merit. Aronson and Mills (1959) observed that, "Persons who go through a great deal of trouble or pain to attain something tend to value it more highly than persons who attain the same thing with a minimum of effort." In this sense, the "initiation" of war—or actual war, even—can leave a lasting and permanent impact.

So, there I was, sitting in my containerized housing unit in full body armor, listening intently. The voices in my head asked if this was worth it, if this was the end, if I had my affairs in order. A lot of things go through the mind of a soldier who has come to terms with the notion that he or she could very well join those three guys— with their hopes and dreams, efforts and toils—among the countless casualties of another pointless war.

Alas, there was little time to waste as the base received the "all clear." The next day, my team was out on patrol in order to not only see if any of the civilian population was willing to share info on what happened, but more importantly, to try to determine *why* it happened. As a Psychological Operations Team Sergeant, my duties involved interacting with the locals via interpreters in an attempt to help persuade, change, and influence the ideas, emotions, and behaviors of our target audience. Our team was a very small cog in a big wheel of the American image. Throughout these daily patrols, I gained a unique insight into the culture of Iraq. I quickly realized how much it differed from what we typically see in our news and entertainment media. This insight turned into appreciation. Only later would it become a viable source of motivation.

It's one thing to see the "have-nots" of the world cope and successfully make a way for their families with nothing but their honor, integrity, and morals. It's quite another thing to come home and see many of the "haves" take many things for granted, at the expense of their honor, integrity and morals. Suddenly, so many things in my life became trivial. I came back from war with a renewed sense of purpose. Oddly enough, this was just the next step in my progression from my earliest days as an HBCU band member.

Upon setting foot on the campus of Hampton University in the fall of 1996, I had no experience with HBCU bands. Needless to say, it came as a bit of a shock. Freshman year challenged my patience, creativity, and ability to accept and overcome adversity. It set me on a path of constant growth and maturity. Before too long, I found my niche in service through music. There's something to be said about taking the time to educate a young mind and then seeing that individual flourish on their own with a sense of accomplishment. To those who do not belong in this field, the process is a drag. To those chosen for this calling, the process is a drug. When you play an active role in building a person and helping them develop a love and passion for music, you want more of that good feeling. The passion becomes a calling, and for the luckiest of us, that calling becomes a career.

So, there I was, sitting in a community center in Brooklyn, New York, surviving on $219 a week and following my calling after leaving Hampton on a leap of faith. Young minds—elementary through high school—with little to no experience, and limited contact with the HBCU world, were finding out that they, too, could attend college through their passion for music. This was in a city that downplayed the importance of the Arts—especially for young people of color—and instead sought to steer these young minds toward vocational careers and away from HBCUs. In all, we were able to send hundreds of students to college who would have otherwise not have attended.

My calling was becoming a career.

After Iraq and a later deployment to Afghanistan, I found myself in Aggieland, in what would prove to be both a daunting challenge and a period of validation. There, at North Carolina Agricultural & Technical State University, I was welcomed with open arms—by most. I was able to do what I loved and what I did while in Brooklyn—music arranging, drill writing, teaching students—now on the collegiate level. More importantly, in addition to teaching, this was the opportunity to truly learn and gain experience. We all face adversity in life. For many of us in the HBCU band world, our experiences have taught us that "running from it will not save you—see it through." There is a special, unique understanding among most HBCU band members: the challenges of band life have prepared us for the challenges of the world. So much so that when a likely drunk fan at a game yelled out to me, "You ain't no real Aggie!" I decided to earn a Ph.D. from North Carolina A&T. Well, maybe that's a simple way of putting it. But hey…

For the luckiest of us, we find ourselves in situations where we not only follow our calling, but we also go where we are called. If nothing else, HBCU bands teach us the value of the occasional leap of faith. The day would eventually come where I got the phone call asking, "So are you going to apply for the job?"

I replied, "What job?"

The North Carolina A&T "Blue and Gold Marching Machine" was riding high and on a continued trajectory upward—and remains so to this day. To then accept the position of Director of Bands at Hampton University and uproot on a whim wasn't an easy decision to make. But somehow, it was. The task was clear: to return to my alma mater and rebuild "The Marching Force" essentially from scratch. In no uncertain terms, it was the mother of all adverse situations.

So, here I am, having helped increase band enrollment from 60 to over 200 members. Here I am, having participated in the Honda Battle of the Bands twice, the New Year's Parade in Rome, and currently bound for the Macy's Thanksgiving Day Parade—all within a span of three years. There is truly something to be said about those of us who have attended an HBCU and those who have participated in an HBCU band. We share a bond, a kinship, and an understanding that we are able to not only face adversity head-on—but to also achieve our goals, no matter how daunting. The fighting spirit of HBCU band members is unlike any other. It is a life-changing experience. As for me—my passion, my calling, my career—the journey continues.

About Thomas L. Jones, Jr., Ph.D.

Dr. Thomas L. Jones, Jr. was born on Clark Air Base in the Philippines and grew up in Texas, New Jersey, South Dakota, North Carolina, and Virginia. Upon graduating from Kecoughtan High School in Hampton, VA, he entered Hampton University on a Presidential Scholarship and Band Scholarship. While at Hampton, he was a member of the band, "The Marching Force," played Trombone and Trumpet, and also served as the Drum Major. He is a charter member of the Pi Beta Chapter of Phi Mu Alpha Sinfonia (Spring 1999), and he is also a Spring 2001 initiate of the Gamma Epsilon Chapter of Omega Psi Phi Fraternity, Inc.

For several years, Dr. Jones served as the music arranger, drill writer, and instructor for the Brooklyn "Steppers" Marching Band, who would go on to win a National High School Marching Band Championship and also appeared in the 2005 Macy's Thanksgiving Day Parade. He would then go on to serve as the Chief Music Arranger, Show Designer, and Media Team Coordinator for the North Carolina A&T State University "Blue and Gold Marching Machine," seeing five appearances at the annual Honda Battle of the Bands, as well as the 2012 Macy's Thanksgiving Day Parade. In August of 2017, Dr. Jones assumed the role as the Director of Bands at Hampton University and led the band to its first ever appearance in the Honda Battle of the Bands in 2018, followed up by an appearance in 2020. The Hampton University band also performed in the 2020 New Year's Day Parade and Celebration in Rome, Italy, and the 2021 Macy's Thanksgiving Day Parade. The band's drumline also performed in the 2019 Tournament of Roses Parade. In his first two years at Hampton University, "The Marching Force" grew from about 60 members to over 200.

In addition to these duties, Dr. Jones also serves in the U.S. Army Reserve. He was deployed to Iraq in 2009-2010 as a Psychological Operations Team Leader, and was also deployed to Afghanistan in 2011-2012 as a Human Terrain Team Research

Manager, and more recently served as a Drill Sergeant in the Army Reserve. Some of his military decorations include the Army Commendation Medal, Commander's Award for Civilian Service, Air Assault Badge, Drill Sergeant Badge, and the Military Outstanding Volunteer Service Medal. He was selected as the 34th Infantry Division Special Troops Battalion Noncommissioned Officer of the Quarter in 2010 and the 4th Psychological Operations Battalion Noncommissioned Officer of the Year in 2011.

Dr. Jones' educational accomplishments are as follows:

- Hampton University, 2009 – BA in General Studies
- Thomas Nelson Community College, 2009 – AS in Science
- Tidewater Community College, 2010 – AAS in Management
- American Military University, 2011 – MS in Space Studies
- Gonzaga University, 2012 – MA in Organizational Leadership
- Pennsylvania State University, 2013 – BS in Psychology
- Liberty University, 2014 – EdS in Educational Leadership
- NC A&T State University, 2014 – PhD in Leadership Studies

Tracey Jackson

The Way of the 100

Tracey Jackson

Florida A&M University

It was August 12, 1997. I wasn't in front of a cake, much less eating a slice of it like I'd done prior on August 12. To add insult to injury, I wasn't even at home, much less in Miami or its surrounding areas. I was an eight-hour, exhausting drive away from home, embarking on my journey to young adulthood. And I couldn't even get a slice of birthday cake on my send off. I spent my 18th birthday away from my family, getting my horn (mellophone, to be exact) and marching band music packet at the Foster-Tanner Music Complex at Florida Agricultural & Mechanical University. Many thoughts ran through my mind. *What am I doing here? Is this what I reeeeaaaaalllllly want to do? Maybe I should call my parents and tell 'em I changed my mind.* But it was too late at that point. They were gone. I stood in the long, carpeted hallway on the fourth floor with my music packet in one hand and mellophone case in the other. It was as if I had been dropped off by a spaceship of freshly graduated high school students on their way to various parts of the country to start their lives.

I chose FAMU and "The Marching 100" as my foray into young adulthood. I lived on a steady diet of this band from my high school band director, Mr. Kenneth Tolbert, who taught at Miami Central, then Miami Norland for many years. He showed us band tapes, pictures of the band, and pictures of him, Dr. White and the Honorable Dr. William P. Foster. He even took us to FAMU's homecoming a few times. But nothing compared to seeing "The 100" in the fall of 1993 as a bright-eyed high school freshman. It was my first school trip out of town. I was drenched in a wet band uniform while enduring cold Tallahassee winds watching "The 100" face off with The Southern University "Human Jukebox". The

Jukebox was known for mercilessly blasting brass wind heavy fanfares and Top 40 tunes all game long.

"The 100" was pure magic in the face of such chaotic excitement. When they played "Endless Love" on the field right before their signature dance routine and exited on "Good Times" amidst thousands of screaming fans, I knew that I just had to "be in that number" and be a FAMU student. Everyone at the game looked smart. They looked like FAMU versions of Whitley, Dwayne Wayne, Kim, Freddie, Ron and the gang from *A Different World*. The FAMU students who came back to my high school to visit Mr. Tolbert, and those who went to my church, came back during the holidays looking grown and accomplished. I wanted in!

Fast forward to Pre-Drill, or what my other friends who marched for other HBCUs called band camp. That warm and fuzzy feeling I felt seeing "The 100" live left my body quickly when I realized it really wasn't the cotton candy experience one hoped for. It was hard work! It was serious business on that practice field referred to as "The Pasture" (a nod to the famous "Patch" rehearsal field that was turned into a retention pond). I, and many of my freshman brothers and sisters, practiced playing and marching with the legends we'd heard about while in high school. Legends who were our mentors and drill sergeants who were soon to graduate and go into the real world. They were not with the foolishness that came with freshmen away from home for the first time, like being late or missing practice because of arbitrary reasons, like hanging out on the student union or oversleeping. It was all business from the moment one walked onto the drill field until the moment practice was over.

For me, every day was a test. Clearly, I wasn't in my right mind. You have to be some level of crazy to want to be a part of "The 100". Between the intense music and field rehearsals, a regular human being will quit after the first day. But there I was, a female brass wind player in a male-dominated section, trying to be "in that number" with so many other hopefuls who dropped like flies, day after day. I had to take everything that was in me to be in this magnificent product.

The culmination of those rough pre-drill rehearsals came down to the very first football game in 90-degree heat against Tennessee State University. No one thinks of putting on a work uniform replete with a base layer that is a sports bra, t-shirt, shorts, socks under said uniform with spats on black shoes, gloves and a shako. No one thinks to wear all of that while performing the infamous "Slow One/Death March" around a regulation-size football field in August. But there I was, wearing said uniform, standing at attention, just like I saw "The 100" do so many times in person and on the video tapes.

The section leader turned around and told us, "Freshmen, for God's sake, do not lock your legs. You'll pass out and fall over!" As quickly as she said it, she quickly disappeared into our rank of mellophone players. Soon after that, the tweet of the whistle from the drum majors entered my ears. Then, the snap from the flag corps and, lastly, the taps of the drum. My left leg immediately went into a 90-degree angle, with my foot perfectly tucked alongside my right leg, just like I practiced so many times in the mirror in my dorm room, at band practice and in sectional rehearsals. I became robotic. It became like clockwork. I became what I saw for some many years instantaneously! My dreams and my reality were in unison at that very moment and thereafter. Game after game, and performance after performance, opponents were crushed. But there was no victory celebration, per se. Just more practice. More perfection. More work to be done. Little did I know that everything I experienced as a freshman then a neophyte member of the most storied black marching band in the country would become a part of the life I live.

Fast forward to the hallowed halls of Corporate America as a software applications designer. Since my career started (and to this day), I've been on various male-dominated teams where I'm the only Black woman. To some, it would be daunting. But to me, it felt natural. That level of comfort was birthed from being one of a few Black women in the male-dominated, brass wind section of "The 100". I've made presentations on some very elaborate software applications I designed. Before entering the room, I'd always tell myself not to lock my knees, just like my section leader said before every performance. After that quick pep talk, I'd simply walk into the boardrooms, ready for battle or simply ready for whatever a C-suite executive decided to throw at me while my manager watched in amazement. I learned that from being in the "100". When projects were performed flawlessly, I began preparing for the next project because I knew that there was always more work to be done. At every life stage in which I found myself, be it on the job, as a member of Zeta Phi Beta Sorority, Inc. and the FAMU National Alumni Association, I execute my duties in the same manner that I executed a field show when I was in uniform and standing in formation with over 300 of my "100" brothers and sisters.

Now that COVID has changed the trajectory of life as we know it, I found solace in cycling. In many ways, while I'm on the open road with my bike club, I find numerous parallels to being in "The 100". Everything I've learned nearly twenty-four years ago on that drill field gets applied whenever I get on my bike in full war regalia (i.e., clip shoes, compression socks, spandex top and shorts, helmet and gloves). Before showtime, I hear the clicks from bike shoes going into pedals and the ticks from wheels spinning instead of the snaps from the flag corps and the taps from the drum corps. Instead of fast marching (i.e., rattling) many steps per minute in straight or variously configured lines for a visual halftime show, it would pedal in straight pacelines that can slice through open roads and snake through corners with ease. I execute gear shifting in unison with my teammates. I'd guide left and right while on the road, just as if I was on the football field. "The 100" is in everything I do since the day my life choices dropped me off in that carpeted hallway on the fourth floor of the Foster-Tanner Music Complex on the campus of Florida Agricultural and Mechanical University.

About Tracey Jackson

Tracey Jackson MBA is a technology professional, author, and speaker.

Tracey is a Jamaican heritaged South Florida native by way of Brooklyn, New York. She is a graduate of Florida A&M University where she earned a bachelor's degree in Computer Information Systems. While at FAMU, Tracey played mellophone in The Incomparable Marching 100 Band and French Horn in the symphonic band for two years. She was also a part of S.I.S.T.U.H.S, a black women's community serviced focused organization where she sat on the leadership team from 2001 to 2002. Prior to graduation, she self-published her first book of poetry called "Impressions" where it was accepted and sold in the university bookstore.

Tracey earned an MBA from Purdue University Global and is currently working as a Senior User Experience Designer where she is a veteran tech conference facilitator. She is also a member of Zeta Phi Beta Sorority Incorporated and is on the executive board of the Miami-Date Chapter of the Florida A&M University Alumni Association. She also is a board member for the faith-based non-profit organization Helping Individuals Succeed.

Tracey has also written several books: From The Valley To The Mountaintop - Lessons from the Journey (Inspirational), The Summer of Chances (full-length African American fiction novel), and "From Yaad" (Caribbean Short themed Novel). She's also written for various newspapers and online magazines.

Official Partners & Sponsors of the HBCU Experience Movement, LLC

Baker & Baker Realty, LLC
Christopher Baker- CEO/Founder
Instagram: seedougieblake
Facebook: Christopher D. Baker
Email: baker.christopher@gmail.com

HBCU Buzz
LUKE LAWAL JR.
lawal@lcompany.co
Fndr, CEO | (301) 221-1719 @lukelawal
L & COMPANY { *HBCU Buzz | Taper, Inc. |
Root Care Health* }

Bound By Conscious Concepts
Kathryn Lomax-CEO/Founder
Instagram: msklovibes223
Facebook: Klo-Kathryn Lomax
Contact: (972) 638-9823
Email: Klomax@bbconcepts.com

Zoom Technologies, LLC
Torrence Reed - CEO/Founder
Instagram: torrencereed3
Email: support@zoom-technologies.co

Dancer NC Dance District
Dr. Kellye Worth Hall
Instagram: divadoc5
Facebook: Kellye Worth Hall
Email: delta906@gmail.com

Yard Talk 101
Jahliel Thurman CEO/Founder
Instagram: YardTalk101
Website: YardTalk101.com

HBCU Wall Street
Torrence Reed & Jamerus Peyton-
CEO/Founders
Facebook: HBCU Wall Street
Email: info@hbcuwallstreet.com

Springbreak Watches (SPGBK)
Kwame Molden- CEO/Founder
Instagram: SPGBK
Facebook: Kwame Molden
Email: info@springbreakwatches.com

Minority Cannabis Business Association
Shanita Penny- President
Instagram- Minority Cannabis
Facebook- MCBA.Org
Twitter- MinCannBusAssoc
LinkedIn- Minority Cannabis Business
Association
Email-info@minoritycannabis.org
Website: www.MinorityCannabis.org
Phone: 202-681-2889

The Phoenix Professional Network image

The Phoenix Professional Network
DJavon Alston-Owner/Founder
Instagram: thephoenixnetwork757
Facebook: DJavon Alston
Email: thephoenixnetwork757@gmail.com

Chef Batts
Keith Batts-CEO/Founder
Instagram: chefbatts
Email: booking@chefbatts.com

Johnson Capital
Marcus Johnson CEO/Founder
Instagram: marcusdiontej
Email: marcus@johnsoncap.com

SheIsMagazine
CEO/Founder: Ciara Horton
Instagram:@sheisemagazine
Facebook:Ciara Horton
Email: ciarasheisemagazine.com

Success and Religion
CEO/Founder: Micheal Taylor
Email: Successismyreligion@gmail.com

Never2Fly2Pray
Jeffrey Lee Sawyer: Owner/Founder
Instagram: never2fly2pray
Facebook: Jeffrey Lee
Email htdogwtr@yahoo.com

Allen Financial Solutions
Jay Allen: Owner/Founder
Instagram: jay83allen
Facebook: Jay Allen
Email: allen.jonathan83@gmail.com

Holistic Practitioners
Tianna Bynum: CEO/Founder
Facebook: Tianna Bynum
Email tpb33@georgetown.edu

Journee Enterprises
Fred Whit: CEO/Founder
Facebook: Fred Whit
Instagram: frederickwjr
Email: frederickwjr@yahoo.com

Queen Series
CEO/Founder: Randall Barnes
Email: aqueenseries@gmail.com

HBCU Girls Talk
CEO/Founder: TeeCee Camper
Instagram: @hbcugirlstalk
Contact: talkgirls@yahoo.com

VJR Real Estate
CEO/Founder: Victor Collins, Jr.
Instagram: vjrtherealtor
Email Address: Vic@TheVJRGroup.com

Company: Ashley Little Enterprises, LLC
Ashley Little- CEO/Founder
Facebook: Ashley Little
Instagram: _ashleyalittle
Email: aalittle08@gmail.com
www.ashleylittleenterprises.com

HBCU Pride Nation
CEO/ Founder: Travis Jackson
Instagram: hbcupridenation
Facebook: HBCU Pride Nation
Email: travispjackson@gmail.com

LK Productions
CEO/Founder: Larry King
Instagram: lk_rrproduction
Facebook: Larry King
Email: lk_production@yahoo.com

STAMP'D TRAVEL
CEO/Founder: Jocelyn Hadrick Alexander
Instagram: @jocehadyou
Website: www.stampdtravel.com
Email Address:
Jocelyn.h.alexander@gmail.com

ICG Marriage & Family Therapy
CEO/Founders: Jabari & Stephanie Walthour
Instagram: @thedopesextherapist
Website: www.intimacycenterga.com
Email Address:
stephanie@intimacycenterga.com

eclectikread
MARKETING

Electikread Marketing
CEO/Founder: Christa Newkirk
Instgram:@chris_ta_da
Email Address: info@eclectikread.com

NXLEVEL TRAVEL (NXLTRVL)
Chief Executive Officer Hercules Conway
Chief Operating Officer Newton Dennis
Instagram-nxlevel
Instagram: herc3k
Facebook-Newton Dennis
Facebook: Hercules Conway
Email Address: info@nxleveltravel.com
Website: NXLEVELTRAVEL.COM

SHANI L.
Relationship Enthusiast
Website: www.shanilfarmer.com
Instagram: @shanilrelationshipenthusiast
Email Address: info@shanilfarmer.com

BLKWOMENHUSTLE
CEO/Founder: Lashawn Dreher
Instagram: blkwomenhustle
Facebook: Blk Women Hustle
Email: info@blkwomenhustle.com

The Alli Group, LLC
Real Estate Management
Lawrence & Nickia Alli
Website: www.thealligroupllc.com
Instagram: @thealligroupllc
Email Address: nickia.alli@gmail.com

HBCU Grad
CEO/Founder Todd Finley
www.hbcugraduates.com
312-535-8511

Upward Path
CEO/Founder: Cameron Chalmers Dupree
Website: www.upwardpathtc.com
Instagram: @upwardpathtc
Email Address: contact@upwardpathtc.com

Campaign
Engineers

Campaign Engineers
Chris Smith, CEO/Founder
Instagram: csmithatl
Email Address: csmith1911@gmail.com

Boardroom Brand LLC
Samuel Brown III, CEO/Founder
Instagram: _gxxdy
Email Address:
samuel.brown.three@gmail.com

HBCU 1010
Jahliel Thurman, CEO/Founder
www.hbcu101.com
Instagram: hbcu101
jahlielthurman@gmail.com

Uplift Clothing Apparel
Jermaine Simpson, CEO/Founder
UpliftClothingApparel.com
Instagram: Upliftclothingapparel

AC Events The Luxury Planning Experience
Amy Agbottah, CEO/Founder:
Email Address: amy@amycynthiaevents.com

The Vernon Group Cooperative Solutions
CEO/Founder: Anthony V. Stevens
Instagram:@investednu
Email Address: info@vernongroupllc.com

LEMM Media Group
CEO/Founder: Cremel Nakia Burney
Instagram: @cremel_the_creator
Email Address: cremelburney@gmail.com

PILAR
Co-Owner: Nate Perry
Instagram: @barpilar
Email Address: nate@pilardc.com

PIXRUS Photo Booth
Natan Mckenzie, CEO/Founder
Email Address: Natan.mckenzie@gmail.com
Instagram: pixrusghana

MMInvestments
Tarik McAllister, CEO/Founder:
Instagram: MMInvestments
Email Address: tarik@mmibuilders.com

AllThingsLoop
Kenya Nalls, CEO/Founder:
Email Address: staff@allthingsloop.com
Contact Number: 773-939-0680

Historically Black Since
CEO/Founder: Adrena Martin
Instagram: historicallyblacksince
www.hbcusince.com

Café Saint Ex
Co-Owner: Nate Perry
Website: www.pilarde.com
Instagram: @barpilar
Email Address: nate@pilardc.com

The Convo with Kisha Podcast
CEO/Founder: Lakisha Mosley
Instagram: @convowithkisha
Email Address: lakisha@lakishamosley.com

Black Women Moguls
CEO/Founder: Averri Liggins
Instagram: @blackwomenmoguls
Email Address:
hello@blackwomenmoguls.com

Hand Made Dreams, LLC
CEO/Founder: Ashley Witherspoon
Instagram: @handmadedreamsllc
Email Address: ashley@handmadedreams.org

HBCU Pulse
CEO/Founder Randall Barnes
Website: hbcupulse.com
Instagram: @hbcupulse
Twitter: @thehbcupulse

According To RP Podcast
CEO/Founder: Ritha Pierre, Esq.
Instagram: @accordingtorp
Email Address: accordingtorp@gmail.com

SwagHer
Vice President Of Sales/Marketing Jarmel
Roberson
Website www.swagher.net
instagram: swaghermagazine
Email Address: jroberson@swagher.net

Freedas World Podcast
CEO/Founder: Ritha Pierre, Esq.
Instagram: @freedas_world
Email Address: accordingtorp@gmail.com

H.E.R. Story Podcast
Janea Jamison|Creator
H.E.R. Story with J. Jamison
#Herstorymovement
IG : @herstory_podcast

HBCU CHEER BLACK EXCELLENCE
Instagram: @HBCUCheer
Email: HBCUcheerleaders@yahoo.com

HBCU Buzz
LUKE LAWAL JR.
lawal@lcompany.co
Fndr, CEO | (301) 221-1719 @lukelawal
L & COMPANY { *HBCU Buzz | Taper, Inc.* |
Root Care Health }

February First
CEO/Founder: Cedric Livingston
www.februaryfirstmovie.com
Director/Writer February First: A Stride
Towards Freedom

The Lady BUGS
CEO/Founder: Tatiana Tinsley Dorsey
Instagram: @theladybugsofficial
Email Address:
ladybugs_HQ@googlegroups.com

HBCU Times
David Staten, Ph.
hbcutimes@gmail.com
Facebook: HBCU Times
Instagram: hbcu_times8892
Bridget Hollis Staten, Ph.D

OEDM Group
CEO/Principal Owner: Justin Blake
Website: www.oedmgroup.com
Instagram: @oedmgroup.com
Email Address: contact@oedmgroup.com

Swing Into Their Dreams Foundation
Pamela Parker and Lynn Demmons, Co-
Founders
Email Address:
swingintotheirdreams@gmail.com
Website: swingintotheirdreams.com

SayYes

Say Yes, LLC
CEO/Founder: Porscha Lee Taylor
Website: www.sayyesplanners.com
Instagram: @sayyesplanners
Email Address: info@sayyescareer.com

Harbor Institute
CEO/Founder: Rasheed Ali Cromwell, JD
Instagram: @theharborinstitute
Facebook: The Harbor Institute
Twitter: @harborinstitute
Email: racromwell@theharborinstitute.com

Marching Sport
CEO/Founder: Gerard Howard
Email Address:
gerardhoward@gmail.com

Vision Tree LLC
CEO/Founder: Dr. Jorim Reed
visiontreellc@gmail.com

THE HBCU
BAND
EXPERIENCE
WITH CHRISTY WALKER

The HBCU Band Experience with
Christy Walker
CEO/Founder: Dr. Christy Walker
Email Address:
christywalker57@gmail.com
Website:
http://www.christyawalker.com

Kelly Collaborative

Kelly Collaborative Medicine
CEO/Founder: Dr. Kathryn Kelly
10801 Lockwood Drive, Suite 160
Silver Spring, MD 20901
(301) 298-1040
www.kellymedicinemd.com

Brooks Arts Collective
LaToya Brooks, Founder
brooksartscollective@gmail.com
IG/FB @brooksartscollective

Reid Creative Solutions, LLC
CEO/Founder: Aja Reid
info@reidcreativesolutions.com
Phone: (919) 822-2892
www.reidcreativesolutions.com

Block Band Music & Publishing, LLC
D. Rashad Watters Founder, CEO
(919)-698-2560
BlockBandMusic@gmail.com

AMMEA
President: Ernest Stackhouse
Email: ej.stackhouse@gmail.com
Website: www.ammea.org

TLW Photography
CEO/Founder: Taylor Whitehead
Email: mrknowitall91@aol.com

SC DJ WORM 803
CEO/Founder: Jamie Brunson
Email: scdjworm803@gmail.com
www.scdjworm803.com
@SCDJWORM803 - Twitter
@SCDJWORM803 - Instagram
SC DJ Worm 803 - Facebook
SC DJ Worm 803 – Mixcloud

The Black Techies/Podcast
CEO/Founder:
Herbert L. Seward III
Slogan: "Where black culture meets the world of technology"
www.theblacktechies.com

themarchingpodcast.com

The Marching Podcast
CEO/Founder: Joseph Beard
Email Address:
marchingpodcast@gmail.com
Website:
www.themarchingpodcast.com

Sugar Top Spirit & Beverage Co
CEO/Founder: Terri White
Email Address:
tl.white412@gmail.com
Website: www.sugartopspirts.com.
Twitter & Instagram
@sugartopspirits

SUPPORT

The Marching Force
www.supportthemarchingforce.com
Mailing address: The Marching
Force - 700 Emancipation Dr.,
Hampton, VA 23668.

PacketStealer Gaming
CEO/Founder: David
Matthews
Email Address:
packetstealer@outlook.com

The Urban Learning &
Leadership Center, Inc.

Urban Learning and Leadership
Center
President and Co-Founder
John W. Hodge, Ed.D
jhodge@ulleschools.com

MilRo Entertainment
Owner: Chevis Anderson
Email: milrosplace@yahoo.com